Trusting God

Trusting God

Learning to Walk by Faith

Dr. David Reagan

Trust in the Lord forever,
for in God the Lord we have an everlasting Rock
— Isaiah 26:4

HUNTINGTON HOUSE, INC.

Shreveport • Lafayette
Louisiana

Dedicated to: Dudley Head, who provided the vision; F.G. "Bob" Yarbrough who gave the leadership; and Bernice Gumm Gammon, who supplied the faith.

Huntington House, Inc.
Lafayette, Louisiana

Typography and cover design by Publications Technologies
Printed in the United States of America

All scripture quotations are from the New American Standard Version, The Lockman Foundation

The poem on page 146, "Epistle" by Carl Sandburg, is taken from *Complete Poems* by Carl Sandburg and is used by permission of Harcourt Brace Jovanovich.

Table of Contents

Part I

The Mission
"Here I am, Lord — Send Someone Else!"

1) Avoiding God

I spent 20 years running as hard as I could from God.

In 1959 when I graduated from the University of Texas, the Lord called me into the ministry. I had gone through college in three years, and I was exhausted. I decided to lay out for a year and work for my dad. I intended to use the time to rest and decide whether I would go to law school or graduate school.

Within a few days after I moved back home, through a bizarre series of circumstances, I found myself the minister of a little country church in Groesbeck, Texas. I knew then that God was calling me to be a minister. But I didn't want to be a minister. I wanted to be a politician. I dreamed of being a governor or U.S. senator. So I rejected the Lord's call, and I rationalized it by saying, "I'll be a politician for Jesus." In reality, I wanted to be a big shot for Dave Reagan.

I served the little country church for a year and then went off to Harvard University to study international politics. Up to that point in my life I had been greatly blessed. I had been born into a Christian family, raised in the church, received an outstanding education and fallen in love with a beautiful Christian girl whom I had married.

7

But when I departed for Harvard, I began running from the Lord, and my fortunes began to change. I failed to earn my master's degree on time because I could not pass the foreign language exam. I had never experienced academic difficulties of any type before in my life, and this failure was a bitter pill. But I was stubborn, and I persisted.

I became one of the first in my class to earn a doctorate. But I found no satisfaction in this accomplishment. In fact, I hated every moment of it. Writing the dissertation was pure drudgery to me, so much so that I have never even looked at it since the day I completed it. It was simply a necessary step in earning a union card for university level teaching — a doctor's degree.

I looked forward to teaching with great enthusiasm, believing that it would fill the vacuum I felt so strongly in my soul. But it didn't. I shifted to a career in academic administration. I thought life would take on new meaning if I could only escape the confinement of the classroom. It didn't.

Finally in 1972 I decided to put the academic life behind me and seek the fulfillment of my childhood dreams. I entered politics. I filed to run for Congress and, again, through a bizarre series of circumstances, I ended up as a candidate for the Republican nomination for governor of Texas! I was only 34 years old. It was a heady experience. It was also a terribly disillusioning experience. I had always been politically motivated by altruistic considerations. I dreamed of honest government that would serve the needs of the people. I found that most people involved in politics are driven by selfish motives. I had my head in the clouds. I spoke of lofty goals like revising the outdated Texas constitution. I discovered that people were more concerned about dollar-and-cent issues.

Once again I tasted the bitterness of failure. I placed third in a field of seven. I railed against God in my heart. "How could He let me down when I wanted to do so much good in His name?"

During the next few years I focused on paying off my campaign debts. I returned to higher education and served as president of one college, dean of another and vice president of a third. I moved almost yearly, giving little consideration to the effect of such a nomadic life upon my wife and two daughters. All that mattered was my career.

I achieved a lot in worldly terms. I held prestigious positions. I made a lot of money. But there was no fulfillment. I continued to feel empty inside.

Then one day I got a brilliant idea. I decided to go into business. My dad was a very successful businessman, and he had urged me for years to get out of the ivory tower and live in the "real world" by starting a business.

It suddenly occurred to me that I could kill two birds with one stone. I could get my earthly father off my back by going into business. At the same time I could get my Heavenly Father off my back by forming a church-related business. I announced I was going to open a Christian book store. It was a pure stroke of genius!

2) Meeting God Halfway

My dad wasn't too excited about the type of business I had in mind. He would have preferred something more down to earth like a plumbing supply distributorship. But he encouraged me to take the step. My younger brother was already a successful businessman. Dad felt that at long last there might be some hope for me!

I was more concerned about the reaction of my Heavenly Father because what I wanted more than anything else in the world was inner peace. I knew that could only come from God.

I didn't know anything in those days about how to seek God's will. I just knew God had called me to be a minister, and I figured that He would jump with joy when I finally stopped running away from Him and took one step in His direction by starting a church-related business. I was wrong. I was to find out the hard way that God is not interested in our meeting Him halfway. He has gone more than halfway in calling us to Him. He expects us to yield fully, not partially, to His will.

I jumped into the project with great enthusiasm. I believed it had to succeed because it had the blessing of both my physical and spiritual fathers.

I spent a year and a half getting the business set up. I had to find a location, purchase a building, secure the fixtures, review the trade magazines and order the stock. It was to be the largest Christian store in Dallas — much more than a mere book store. We were going to offer Christian music, Bible school curriculum, religious art, church supplies, choir robes, fiberglass baptistries — you name it. During the year and a half it took to get the business started I had no income. My wife and I sold every asset we had, including our house, to generate the money necessary for such a grandiose business. What we couldn't afford, we secured through loans granted on my dad's credit. It never occurred to me to start small and grow. No, my store had to be the biggest and the best.

I called it Renewal House. The name proved prophetic, for God used it to renew me.

I operated the store for a year and a half. Our volume of business grew steadily each month, but never fast enough. There was too much overhead and too much interest on loans. Finally, the day arrived when I had no operating cash left. I called the bank for more. The answer was "No!"

I'll never forget that day. Three years of my life — every waking moment — had gone into this project. Now I faced bankruptcy. Failure again. It was more than I could bear. I became physically ill. I descended into a pit of depression.

A few days later I had to put the "CLOSED" sign on the front door. That was a tough moment. I looked out the window at the homosexual bar that was located right across the street from my store. The place had standing-room-only every night. The money was rolling in. I wanted to scream, "Why me God? Why not that den of iniquity?" Just then the owner of the bar drove up in his four-door Jaguar and parked out front. He was wearing an expensive looking suit. He stood by his car for a moment, lighting a cigar. It was as if Satan was taunting me, saying, "Look how I reward those who serve me!"

The emotional distress intensified later that day when I called the bank to get the total on how much I owed. The answer blew me away: "Your loan balance is $100,000." One hundred thousand dollars! I could not even imagine that much money. Where would I get it? How could I avoid bankruptcy and total humiliation?

3) Limiting God

I desperately needed God. But I didn't know how to reach out to Him.

I had grown up in a legalistic and sectarian church. We believed we were the only ones who had the truth. We believed the rest of the so-called "Christian world" was terribly deceived. We consigned them to hell and believed they deserved it because, after all, they didn't agree with us!

We believed the Bible was the Word of God, but we did not believe in the God who was revealed in the Bible. Our God was a God of Nostalgia. He was the "Grand Old Man in the Sky." He was a God who once performed mighty deeds in Old Testament and New Testament times — but who ran out of gas at the end of the First Century. He had gone into retirement. The age of miracles had ceased.

If I wanted to experience God, I had to go see a movie like *The Ten Commandments,* in Technicolor and Panavision, with a cast of thousands. I would sit there in awe as I witnessed Cecil B. DeMille re-create the miracles of God dividing the Red Sea, leading the Children of Israel with a cloud and feeding them with manna. I would drive home with goose bumps, yearning for such a God today — a God of power who was concerned about me and my problems.

But I didn't believe in such a God. My God was an impersonal God who had more important things to worry about than my problems. Furthermore, even if He were concerned, He couldn't do anything because He no longer intervened in human affairs — except, of course, to bug me to preach!

My church had rejected more than the power of God. We had set aside the whole realm of the supernatural. We did not believe in demons or angels. They too had retired at the end of the First Century!

We knew nothing about spiritual warfare. We thought our battle was with flesh and blood. We knew nothing about the power of the Word, the power of prayer or the power of the name of Jesus.

Our faith was all past tense — directed at the Cross. Our faith did not relate to the present or the future. Regarding the present, our attitude was that God had given us a rule book and minds. We were to follow the rules and use our minds to cope rationally with the problems of life.

Our faith did not relate to the future because we ignored God's prophetic Word. Also, we were caught up in works salvation, and therefore we were all uncertain about our eternal destiny. The future was unknown. We tried not to think about it.

Our faith was really in our church. We trusted in the church because we were told that our church was right about everything. We took pride in our church. We took glee in putting down other churches.

We were debaters. We liked to prove that other people were wrong. By age 15 I had pages in the back of my Bible that were designated for every major denominational group. On each page I had a list of proof texts that I used to attack that particular group. We had a zeal to prove we were right about everything.

This was before the days of Christian radio and television and Christian bookstores. We could keep our people in isolation from the rest of the world. We talked only to ourselves.

Another aspect of our rejection of the supernatural was our treatment of the Holy Spirit. We mainly ignored the Spirit. Our preachers felt that any emphasis on the Spirit would lead to "dangerous emotionalism." The Holy Spirit was the great taboo topic of our fellowship.

This caused me some real problems as a child. The only version of the Bible that we used was the King James. It used the term "Holy Ghost." That was confusing to me. I felt like the Holy Ghost was supposed to be something good, but all the ghosts I had ever heard about had been evil. I would go on Boy Scout camp outs and we would sit around the campfire at night and tell ghost stories. We were good at it because we would all end up sleeping in the same tent!

I kept asking myself how a ghost could be good. One Saturday morning when I was about 12 years old I found the answer. I got on the city bus in Waco, Texas where I grew up and went downtown to the Strand Theatre where I paid 9 cents to see a cowboy double feature. Between the features they stuck in a serial and a cartoon.

As I watched the cartoon that morning, my theology of the Holy Ghost suddenly crystallized. The cartoon was "Casper, the Friendly Ghost." It dawned on me that the Holy Ghost is like Casper — always there to help you out, to pick you up, dust you off, encourage you and help you win your battles.

I didn't have any more trouble with the Holy Ghost until I was 16. At that age all the boys in my church went through a rite of passage called "Young Men's Bible Training Class." We were taught how to pray, teach, serve communion and prove that a Methodist was going to Hell.

I caused quite a stir the night we studied the Holy Ghost. The teacher began by asking, "Who can identify the Holy Ghost?" I jumped at the opportunity. "The Holy Ghost," I blurted out, "is like Casper, the Friendly Ghost!" I almost received the left foot of fellowship that night. The teacher turned me every way but loose. He told me in no uncertain terms that Casper had nothing to do with the Holy Ghost. "The Holy Ghost," he explained, "is the Bible."

That's right. We were taught that the Holy Spirit is an inanimate object — a book. If we wanted to get the Spirit, we would have to memorize the book. The more we learned, the more of the Spirit we would receive.

4) Reaching Out to God

The point is that as I stood there that day in the mid-70s facing the chilling reality of a failed business and a $100,000 debt, I had no inner spiritual power to help me cope with the crisis.

Let me take that back. I did have the power, for I had received Jesus as my Savior many years before, and on that day I had received the indwelling power of His Spirit. There was power within me in the form of God's Spirit. But I didn't know that. I had never plugged into the power. I had never released the power of the Spirit in my life. Instead, I had stifled and quenched the Spirit. I thought the Spirit was a book. I did not realize that the Spirit is a personality, that the Spirit is the supernatural presence of God in the world today and that He dwells within believers.

I could recite the five steps in what our church called "The Plan of Salvation." I could also recite what we called "The Five Acts of Worship." I could give you chapter and verse to substantiate 25 of our pet doctrines. But I had no power to cope with a business failure and a $100,000 debt.

So I did the only thing I knew how to do — I threw a pity party. I wallowed in self-pity. And as I did so, I sank deeper into the pit of depression.

I finally became so despondent that I decided to kill my self. I felt like I just couldn't face the disgrace and pain of such a failure. Also, I was mad at God. How could He let me down so miserably when I had, at long last, deigned to meet Him halfway? In my emotionally perverted reasoning, I decided that by taking my life I would teach God a lesson! I know that sounds weird, but when you are deeply depressed, you don't think too clearly.

For several days I plotted my demise. Just as I had everything carefully planned, I suddenly got a strange thought: "Why not try God?" That was a strange thought for me because I didn't believe in either a personal or a powerful God. Looking back on it today I can only conclude that the thought must have come from the stirring of the Spirit within me. I had quenched the Spirit, but the Spirit was still there and, like Casper, He was trying to minister to me in my time of need.

I tried to suppress the thought, but it would not go away. Over and over it came to me: "Why not try God?"

I finally decided to follow the prompting. I got on the phone and called several friends. I asked them to come to my house. When they arrived, I explained my predicament and asked them to pray for me. One by one they prayed. Their prayers were lifeless and unbelieving. They no more believed in a personal and powerful God than I did.

As the prayers droned on, I became agitated. "This won't do," I interrupted. "None of you are praying with any meaning. You don't understand, I need a miracle! Let's try again and this time, pray with some faith!" I could hardly believe those words came out of my mouth. But they did. My friends started praying again, this time with some fervor.

God performed the miracle the very next morning, and it transformed my life. You could start guessing right now and guess till the Lord returns, and you would never guess how God answered our prayers.

You see, when God responds to a cry for help, He does so in a manner that is always designed to minister first to the inner man, to the spiritual nature. It's not that He's unconcerned about the physical man and the physical and emotional pain. It's just that His priorities are different from ours. We want to be ministered to from the outside in. He ministers from the inside out, because that is the only kind of ministry that has lasting effects.

If you were to guess how the Lord answered our prayers, you would most likely assume that some man walked in my store the next morning and offered me $100,000 for the business. That would have been truly remarkable, but it would not have had a transforming effect on me. I would probably have written it off to "coincidence" rather than recognizing it as an answer to prayer. Most likely I would have sighed with relief and gone on my way continuing to try to meet God halfway.

God answered my prayer miraculously, but He did it in a way designed to get my attention, to convince me that He truly is a personal and powerful God who is on the throne, hears prayers and still performs miracles. He also used a method that was designed to transform me more into the image of His Son.

5) A Transforming Miracle

Here's what happened. The next morning I went to the store and started calling around trying to find a buyer for my fixtures. I was standing at the front counter talking on the phone when I heard a knock at the front door. I turned and looked at the plate glass door and saw an oriental man and woman standing there. The man was grinning from ear to ear. I pointed to the sign hanging on the door and turned my back on the couple. The sign said, "CLOSED: Going Out of Business."

The man resumed his knocking. I got mad. Couldn't this fellow read? Why did he have that big grin on his face? The last thing I wanted to see was someone happy. Misery really does love company.

I put the phone down, went to the door, opened it about an inch and shouted, "Can't you read? We're closed!"

"Oh yes sir," he replied, "I know you are closed. I'm interested in buying your fixtures."

"Oh!" I replied. "Come in. Come in."

I locked the door and went back to the phone while the oriental man and lady looked around the store. When I finished talking, the man came up to me, still grinning, and said, "Thank you, dear sir, for letting me see your store." He was almost nauseating in his politeness. He continued to grin and started bowing in the oriental style. Then he started apologizing! "I'm very sorry, dear sir, but you do not have any fixtures I'm interested in. I'm opening up a different type of store."

I escorted him and the lady to the door. The lady walked out, but as the man got halfway through the door, he suddenly stopped, turned to me and said, "I discern that you are troubled in the spirit. Do you want to talk about it?"

Talk about getting angry. I was livid. Who did this guy think he was? I replied in my "best" Christian manner, "What's it to you?"

"Well," he replied, "I assume from the nature of this store that you must be a Christian. I am too. And I discern that you need ministry. Would you mind if I shared with you what Jesus Christ has done for me in my life?"

I didn't want to hear his story. I wanted him to leave. But what was I to say? It was like when someone asks if they can pray for you. You may not want them to but you hate to say no.

"I'm awfully busy," I said, as I glanced at my watch in irritation.

"It won't take but a moment," he replied. He grinned again.

"OK, OK," I said, "but make it quick."

He turned and said something to the lady in a foreign language, and she left. I locked the door again, and we went to my office. When we sat down on the couch, he put his arm around me and began to pat my shoulder sympathetically. Again, I was outraged. Who does this guy think he is? He hardly knows me, and he has his arm around me.

But I soon forgot my anger as he began to tell his story.

"When I was a small boy, my father came home one day with terror in his eyes. 'The Communists are coming,' he said, 'and they are going to kill us because we are devout Catholics.'

"He told each of us to get two pillow slips and to go to the living room. He started running all over the house gathering up items which he piled in the middle of the floor. 'Put these in the pillow slips,' he said, 'and tie the tops.'

"We were a very wealthy family, but all we took with us that day was what we could stuff into those pillow slips. We fled into the jungle, and we threw ourselves upon the Lord because we didn't know how to survive in the jungle. There were 12 of us in all. We wandered about aimlessly crying out to God to save us.

"Finally, after three weeks, we made it from Hanoi to Saigon, and we rejoiced over the Lord's deliverance.

"We began our life anew. Many years later I came home one day to my family and my aged parents with that same look of terror in my eyes. 'Get the pillow slips,' I yelled. 'The Communists are coming again.'

"I was a translator at the American Embassy. I had been informed that the Embassy could not arrange for all my family to be flown out. I would not leave without them. So, once again, we had to flee. I knew if we stayed we would be executed because I had worked for the Americans.

"We fled into the Mekong Delta and, again, we began to cry out to God for deliverance. After wandering for several days, we made it to the South China Sea where we discovered a boat full of refugees about to depart. God had saved us a second time!

"But when the boat got out to sea, it started sinking. There were just too many people on it. Some people panicked and began to push others overboard. Some even threw their children into the sea. We got on our knees and started calling out to God. Soon, a merchant ship appeared and took the survivors on board. God had saved us a third time!

"We were taken to the Philippines where we were put with

thousands of other refugees in a concentration type camp. We began praying that God would give us a new home. A year later the news came that we were being adopted by a Bible Church in Dallas, Texas. God saved us a fourth time.

"So, here we are in a new land starting our lives over. God is so good. He loves us, and He answers our prayers. Lean on Him. He will deliver you."

I looked at the man with tears in my eyes. Before I knew it, I had my arms around him, hugging him in thankfulness for insisting on sharing a story I had not wanted to hear.

When he left, everything had changed. Yet, nothing visible had changed. I still had a failed business. I still owed a bank $100,000. What had changed was me. I no longer felt depressed. I was no longer wallowing in despair and self-pity. I had hope. I knew in my soul that God had heard my prayer and that He had sent that man to assure me that if I would trust in the Lord, everything would turn out all right. God had used an oriental man from halfway around the world to get my eyes off myself and onto His Son.

I had no problems compared to the problems that man had faced. If God could solve his problems, He surely could handle mine.

6) *Discovering God*

God had gotten my attention, but He did not yet have *me*.

During my years of running from the Lord, I had developed many sinful attitudes, thoughts and habits. I was in bondage to pride and lust. I wrestled daily with a hot temper. I still dreamed of worldly success.

I still had a long way to go before I could become a useful servant of the Lord's. I had to get to know God as a personal, caring and powerful God. I had to get to know myself — to

really know myself — by honestly facing up to my faults. I had
to learn how to surrender myself to God's will and then how to
live on the power of His Spirit rather than the power of my
flesh.

The Lord began the process by giving me an insatiable appe-
tite for His Word. I had grown up in a Bible believing church.
Theologically we proclaimed the Bible as the revealed Word of
God, and we stood on the authority of the scriptures. But in
practice, we put our traditions above the Word. We played
games with Scripture.

When the Word contradicted our doctrines, we either spiritualized the passage or we dispensationalized it. We spiritualized
by saying that the passage didn't mean what it said. We dispensationalized by arguing that the passage had ceased to be valid at
the end of the First Century.

We also tended to use the Bible as a debating handbook.
Rather than reading it to seek truth or simply to allow the Holy
Spirit to minister to our hearts, we approached it as though it
were the Texas Code Annotated. We looked for proof texts to
justify our doctrines and to prove others wrong.

As I started reading the Bible anew, the Spirit led me to read it
in a different way. Rather than searching for proof texts, I found
myself reading for the sheer joy of it. As I read, I began to make
some amazing discoveries. For example, prophecy began to
make sense, if I would just believe what it said.

In fact, the whole Bible began to make more sense to me as I
began to accept what it said as meaning what it said and as being
applicable to me today. As a trained academic, I had always approached the Bible as literature to be analyzed, categorized and
theologized. I now became aware that it was written to be believed and acted upon.

It was difficult, but I began to put aside the rationalizing, the
spiritualizing and the dispensationalizing. As I did so, I found
that the Word began to transform me. For the first time my eyes
were opened to my own faults rather than the faults of others.
Time and time again I was brought to my knees in repentance.

The Word became a spiritual mirror reflecting my inadequacies compared to the perfection of Jesus.

I also began to discover some important things about God. First and foremost was the revelation that He is the same yesterday, today and forever (Mal. 3:6 and Heb. 13:8). What a discovery that was for me! God had not retired! He is alive and well. He is still the same God as the one revealed in the Bible — a God who is sovereign, personal, loving, caring, powerful and who still intervenes in history in response to the faith of those who seek Him. I could hardly contain my joy.

The Word was not my only teacher during those difficult days following my business failure. I was also shaped and molded by the Lord's discipline.

After I sold off all the assets of the business, I still owed the bank $60,000. I negotiated a deal to pay off that debt by agreeing to pay the bank a minimum of $1,000 a month. That obligation meant that my family and I were going to have to learn to live on a greatly reduced income. Our whole lifestyle was transformed almost overnight.

Prior to the business failure, my income had been increasing rapidly almost every year. But like most Americans captivated by materialism, no matter how much I made, it was not enough. I always needed a bigger house or a larger car. Suddenly, we had to learn how to live a frugal lifestyle. All I earned each month went to pay off the debt. So we lived on my wife's income as a first grade teacher.

It was the discipline of the Lord. It wasn't easy, but it was another spiritually transforming experience. We were delivered from materialism. We learned how to live simply, how to count our blessings, how to be satisfied with what we had. We began to learn about how to trust in the Lord to provide our basic needs.

But we were still pretty much what I would call "Cultural Christians." By that I mean that my wife and I had been born into Christian families, raised in the church and considered Christian values to be an integral part of our lives. We attended church regularly and made sure that our children were involved in all the church's activities. In short, we were a typical American church-going family.

The problem with that is that we were not committed disciples of the Lord. Like most Christians, we had accepted Jesus as Savior but not as Lord. We had received His Spirit into our lives, but we had never released the power of the Spirit. For me the Spirit was a resident but not president. He resided but He did not preside. My ego was on the throne of my life.

I still needed a lot of the Lord's discipline. I began to taste it when I decided to take one more step in the direction of the Lord's will for my life. I had been preaching part time on the weekends for a church in Irving, Texas. When the business collapsed, they asked me to become their full time pastor. I agreed.

At long last, I had given in to the Lord's will for my life. I expected to be blessed mightily. I looked forward to receiving the inner peace that I so desperately desired. I was in for a surprise.

I was to learn that the Lord could not minister effectively through me because I still had not surrendered myself to Him. I had surrendered my career but not my self. I still had a lot of sin in my life that I refused to deal with. I still wanted to run the show my way.

I tried to run the church like I would run a university or a business. I set goals, organized committees and attempted to manipulate people to do what I wanted. I was involved in constant confrontations.

I was not filled with the Spirit. I did not know anything about spiritual gifts. I operated in the flesh. It was all I knew how to do.

God in His mercy blessed me in many ways during the three chaotic years that I served that church. As I said before, He got me immersed in the Word. He began to open my eyes to the things of the Spirit. He began to deal with the sin in my life. Through all the conflict, He taught me more about Himself, myself and other people.

Near the end of that ministry I tasted the discipline of the Lord again in a traumatic event involving our younger daughter. She became involved with drugs. Her whole personality changed. She became moody and tempestuous. Her school work declined. Family arguments grew more frequent. All the signs of drug involvement were there, but we didn't recognize them. We could not begin to conceive that a child of ours could be having a drug problem. That was the kind of nightmare that afflicted other families, not ours.

But it did afflict us. One day it culminated with our daughter running away from home. She was only 16. She vanished completely. For three months we did not know if she was dead or alive.

During those awful days of waiting and wondering — days of weeping and searching — Satan attacked us with everything he could use. We were overwhelmed by self-condemnation. We felt judged and censured by some of our friends. Every news report seemed to contain a horror story about the mutilation death of a runaway. A special television documentary on runaways indicated that most girls end up as prostitutes.

We felt totally helpless. In our helplessness, we turned to God as never before. My wife and I joined hands and got on our knees and cried out to God for mercy. We admitted our inability to cope with the situation and, like little children, we cried out to our Father for help.

As we emptied ourselves and humbled ourselves before the Lord, we experienced the filling of His Spirit. We received a peace that was beyond human understanding. We felt assured that our daughter was in His hands and that everything would turn out OK if we would only lean on the power of His Spirit and trust in His mercy.

My wife and I were drawn closer to each other. Long lingering resentments evaporated. Pettiness dissipated. Love was renewed. God was working mightily through a tragedy to heal our marriage and to renew and deepen our relationship with Him.

Our daughter was found alive and well, living and working in a small town in Indiana. We had walked through the valley of the shadow of death and found that the Lord walks with you every step of the way if you will only let Him.

My experience with the filling of the Spirit motivated me to launch an intensive study of the Holy Spirit and spiritual gifts. It did not take me long to discover that I did not have the spiritual gifts to be a pastor. I did not have a pastor's heart. I did not have the love and patience to shepherd a flock of God's people.

By the time I made that discovery, I was already burned out from operating in the flesh and terribly confused. Why had God called me into the ministry without giving me the gifts to be an effective minister? I just couldn't figure it out.

I had run from the Lord as hard as I could run for almost 20 years. Then, when I stopped running and gave into His will, He allowed me to fail again. Was He some sort of cosmic sadist?

I decided to chuck the whole thing. I resigned in disgust and returned to my career in higher education, accepting a position as vice president for development for a private, church-related university in Oklahoma. I decided that I had misread God. I hadn't. God had simply been trying to teach me some things that I desperately needed to know if I was ever to be an effective servant of His. Now He was preparing to put me through a wilderness experience that was designed to move me into the center of His will.

7) *Wrestling with God*

Although the job I had been offered was an outstanding one, I had some strong reservations about it. The university was related to a denomination that had a very liberal reputation. I could not get excited about raising money to assist the propagation of theological liberalism.

I raised this point with the new president of the university who had offered me the job. He assured me that the school did not share the liberal viewpoint of the denomination that supported it. "We are located in a conservative area," he pointed out, "and we must maintain a conservative posture if we are to attract the support of our surrounding churches."

I was soon to discover that in religion, as in politics, the terms "conservative" and "liberal" are highly subjective. I quickly realized that what the university president considered "conservative" was to me nothing but rank liberalism.

Because I was suspicious from the start, I refused to move my family to Oklahoma. I decided to get an apartment and check out the situation. For the next six months I lived alone, commuting to Dallas on weekends.

I did not realize it at the time, but God had maneuvered me into exactly the place where He wanted me — alone and isolated. He was determined to get my undivided attention. He had set me up for a wilderness experience.

Disillusionment with the new job set in almost the moment I arrived on campus. The school had been thoroughly secularized. It was church-related in name only. Religion professors openly scoffed at the Bible. Fundamentalists were ridiculed. My worst suspicions proved true.

I was bewildered again. Why had God led me to this place? I was bordering on despair when I decided to go to my knees. I began to pray with a zeal I had never before experienced. Every night I poured my heart out to God. "Oh Lord, why am I here? I'm so lonely, so empty, so confused. What is your will for me? What must I do to receive peace? Have mercy upon me, Oh Lord. Have mercy. Show me what you want me to do. I'm tired of running from You. I'm weary of being out of Your will. Close all the doors You do not want me to go through. Leave open only the door You want me to enter, and then give me the courage and faith to go through it. Please, dear God, show me Your will!"

Night after night I continued to pray and weep before the Lord. Finally, one night I became so exhausted that I shut up and simply knelt by my bed in silence. It was then that I heard the voice of God — not audibly. It was His Spirit witnessing to mine. The message was clear and precise: "Resign your job. Step out in faith and preach 'Jesus is coming soon.' Preach 'Flee from the wrath that is to come.'"

It was a "good news, bad news" message for me. The good news was the call to preach the soon coming of Jesus. The Holy Spirit had led me into an intensive study of Bible prophecy that had brought me to the conclusion that we are living in the season of the Lord's return. The message was heavy on my heart. In fact, like Jeremiah, it was burning in my breast (Jer. 20:9). It was a message I ardently wanted to proclaim.

The bad news was that the Lord wanted me to do it by faith. That scared me to death. I had taught a lot about faith and preached faith. But I never really had done anything by faith. I discovered there is a great leap from preaching to doing.

So, instead of saying, like Isaiah, "Here am I, Lord, send me," I began to make excuses like Moses did when he said, "Here am I, send Aaron." I waffled all over the place.

"But Lord," I said, "how will I support myself? I'm still paying on my business debt. And I've got a daughter about to start to college. How will I pay her tuition?"

Excuse followed excuse. I pelted the Lord with questions. The only answer I received was a command: "Resign your job. Step out in faith and preach 'Jesus is coming soon.' Preach 'Flee from the wrath that is to come.'"

The Lord wasn't interested in my questions. His only concern was my obedience.

But I wasn't ready to obey. I wanted to wrestle. I tried my old ploy of compromise. "OK, Lord," I said, "I'll meet you halfway. I'll find a church where I can preach. That way I'll have an assured income. Then I will go out during the week to other churches and proclaim the soon return of Your Son."

The Lord wasn't impressed. His only response was a question: "Is that faith?" I knew it wasn't. But I didn't have the faith to do what He wanted me to do. I continued to wrestle with Him.

As I look back on that wrestling match and consider my incredible stubbornness and lack of faith, I can only praise God that He is so patient and full of lovingkindness. Instead of washing His hands of me in disgust, He began to give me supernatural confirmation of His will for my life. That confirmation was to radically change my life, propelling me into the center of His will.

8) Surrendering to God

One day in the midst of all this spiritual struggle, I went to the mail box and discovered a package from an old friend in Houston. Inside was a cassette tape by Pat Robertson. The topic was "How to Seek the Guidance of God." I later learned it was one of a series of 12 tapes Robertson had done on spiritual guidance. Through my friend, God had selected this one tape for me to hear. The note that came with the tape simply said: "While I was listening to this tape, God impressed upon my heart to send it to you."

The topic and timing of the tape intrigued me. I listened to it immediately. In the middle of the tape Robertson suggested that if you are ever struggling with a career decision and you think you've heard God's voice as to what you are to do, you might put the guidance you have received to a spiritual test by using the Old Testament principle of seeking the confirmation of two or more witnesses. That advice witnessed to my spirit and I decided to follow it that moment.

I picked up the phone and called one of the godliest men I knew in Dallas. "Bob," I said, "you may think I'm crazy but I believe God has called me to resign my job and step out in faith and preach the soon coming of Jesus."

"That's great!" he replied. "What can I do to help?"

"I want you to pray about it for three days," I said. "Then call me back and tell me what the Lord has spoken to your heart."

He agreed. The three days seemed to drag by as I waited anxiously for his call.

Promptly on the evening of the third day Bob called back.

"Dave," he said, "you'd better sit down."

"What do you mean?"

"I mean God has given a strong and clear answer to my prayers. You're not going to believe what has happened."

My heart began to pound, and I sat down.

"First of all," he said, "God has really impressed upon me in my prayers that you are to take this step of faith. Second, I have mentioned the matter to only two people and yet, in three days' time, I have spontaneously received commitments from people all over Dallas who have pledged to give $800 a month for the first year!"

I was stunned. This was far beyond anything I had imagined. I didn't know what to say. Talk about God hitting you over the head with a baseball bat! It was like He was screaming from the heavens, "Do it, David!"

Then Bob asked, "Are you going to do it?"

I should have been rejoicing, but I was frightened. I started scrambling for excuses.

"Well, Bob, I just don't know yet. You see, I'm running an experiment. I'm seeking confirmation from two witnesses. You're the first. I have to find another."

I thanked him for calling and hung up. I was scared — really scared. I had put God to the test and He had come through with flying colors. The ball was in my court.

I decided I needed to give the whole matter some careful thought. I put off seeking the second witness for several days. During that time I kept searching through my mind, trying to come up with the name of the second person I would call. I made list after list of names. I kept ruling out people for various reasons. "This one won't be honest with me. That one will tell me what he thinks I want to hear. I can't call her because she won't really pray about it." On and on the excuses went.

As I look back on that selection process today, it is clear that the real reason I ruled out so many people is because I was afraid they would confirm God's call. I was searching for some one who would say, "You're crazy — forget it."

The ideal person who finally came to mind was a lady named Bernice. She was a widow in her late 70s who lived in Dallas. I had known her for about three years., though not well. Most of my contact with her had been through letters and telephone conversations.

But I knew her well enough to know that she was a goldplated character. Somehow, she always managed to get a tape recording of every sermon I delivered in the Dallas area. She would listen to the sermon and then send me a five-page, single-spaced, typed letter in which she would take the sermon apart paragraph by paragraph. "Your introduction was weak. You should have used a different scripture to back up your point. You misused the scripture you quoted. You mispronounced the prophet's name." She was a real burr under my saddle. I felt like she was my self-appointed spiritual watchdog.

She was even more peculiar over the phone. She would answer gruffly with a phrase I could never understand. The words all ran together in what sounded like a command of a top sergeant. Finally, one day I got up enough nerve to ask her what she always shouted when she answered the phone. "I've never been able to understand what you say when you answer the phone," I explained. "Could you say it slower?"

"Of course," she replied in an irritated manner. "I say 'Rejoice in the Lord always.' And you are supposed to reply, 'And again, I say rejoice!' "

At long last I realized why our phone conversations always got off to a bad start. I didn't complete the scripture verse that she was shouting at me!

Bernice never had time for pleasantries on the phone. If I asked, "How are you doing?" she would likely reply, "Not so hot. What do you want?" She was always anxious to get to the bottom line. One never knew when she might terminate the conversation. When she got tired of talking, she would just hang up, often without even bothering to say good-bye.

Needless to say, I always got nervous when Bernice called me. I knew I was in trouble. So when I thought of her as the second possible witness, I did not relish the idea of calling her. But I knew she would shoot straight with me, and I felt it was likely that she would say, "You're nuts!"

"Hello Bernice, this is David."

"David who?"

"David Reagan"

"What do you want?"

We were off to a great start. I could tell she was annoyed by my call. I had caught her in a particularly bad mood. I was delighted. I felt sure this would be the end of my grand experiment.

I related the message I felt God had laid on my heart.

"Why are you telling me this?" she snapped.

"Because I want you to pray about it," I explained. "Pray about it for three days and then let me know what you think the Lord wants me to do."

"OK, I'll do it." She hung up.

No goodbye.

I smiled and thought, "That's the end of that." But I was in for a big surprise from the Lord.

Three days later Bernice called back. She spoke like a person transformed. No gruffiness. No staccato commands. I could hardly believe it was her.

She was excited. "David, you're not going to believe what has happened!"

"What?" I asked, now frightened by her positive tone and obvious enthusiasm.

"Well, first of all, God has really confirmed your call in my prayers. There's no doubt about it! And guess what? I've received an inheritance of $3,000 since you called. And if you will resign and start the new ministry, I will give you $1,000 of my inheritance."

Never in my life had I been so stunned. Could this really be Bernice? Was she really speaking words of encouragement? Had I heard her correctly? Did she just offer me one-third of her inheritance?

I don't know how long I stood there in stunned silence, but I was brought back when I heard her shout, "David, are you still there? Speak to me!"

"Yes, Bernice, I'm still here. It's just that I'm sort of flabbergasted by all this."

"Well, I've got more good news," she said. "Aren't you driving a university car?"

"Yes."

"Won't you need a car in the ministry?"

"Yes."

"Well, I've got one for you!"

That's when I nearly lost it. I dropped into a chair and just sat there limp. Then I heard something really strange. Laughter. Yes, Bernice was laughing! I didn't even know she knew how!

"What are you laughing about?" I asked.

"Well," she paused and giggled like a little child, "don't get too excited about the car. You see, it's a holy car."

"A holy car? What's a holy car?"

"It's one that's been prayed over on the side of the road many times!"

In short, it was an old junker. But that was irrelevant. The only thing that mattered at the moment was the fact that God had motivated this grand old lady to give me a car and part of her inheritance.

"Are you going to do it?" she asked.

Again, incredibly, I waffled. Again, God had hit me over the head with a two by four to get my attention. What more confirmation could a person ask for? But I was scared and just didn't have the faith to take the step.

"I'm running an experiment," I lamely explained. "I'll call you back in a few days."

I was sharing this story recently with an Episcopal priest friend of mine. When I got to this point in the story, he stopped me and said, "I'll bet I know what you did next."

"How do you know?" I asked.

"Because I've been there."

"OK," I said, "tell me what I did next."

"Well, being the great man of faith that you are, I figure you got on your knees and asked God for a third witness."

"You've definitely been there," I replied.

I'm ashamed to admit it but that's exactly what I did. "Lord," I cried out, "you've overwhelmed me with these two confirmations. But Lord, I may have stacked the deck. I may have called people I knew would say, 'Yes.' Lord, I want to make certain of Your will. So, Lord, if You really want me to do this, then You send a third witness — an unsolicited witness. If You'll do that, Lord, I'll take the step of faith."

I was still playing games with God. I knew I hadn't "stacked the deck." The Lord's will for me had been confirmed. I was just scared and kept pointing to my precarious financial situation — the need to pay off the debt and the need to send my daughter to college.

But there was a deeper fear that I didn't want to admit because it was rooted in pride. My greatest fear was what people would think of me.

After all, I was a distinguished academician with a doctorate from a Harvard graduate school. I knew what sort of things people would say about a fellow — any fellow — who suddenly started preaching the soon return of Jesus. Both family and friends would write me off as a candidate for the guys with the butterfly nets.

So I squirmed and made excuses. I sought a third witness.

Any other god would have zapped me with a lightening bolt. But the God I was dealing with was the God who is full of patience and longsuffering. He continued to prod me like a little child.

The very next morning after talking to Bernice and praying for another confirmation, God sent the third witness. He came in a most unusual form, and I learned that when you are seeking God's guidance, you should be sensitive to receiving it from strange sources.

The witness was one of the greatest preachers of this century, Dr. Martin Lloyd-Jones. No, he didn't appear at my door. At least, not in person. God sent him to me through a magazine article.

The next morning I received in the mail the latest issue of *Christianity Today*. On the cover was a drawing of Dr. Jones. I didn't know much about him, but what I knew really intrigued me. I knew he had written several volumes on the book of Romans which had received worldwide acclaim. He had the reputation of being the foremost expository preacher in all of Christendom.

I decided to read the article before going on to the office. The occasion of the article was Dr. Jones' 80th birthday. It took the form of an interview:

Question: "What seminary did you attend?"

Answer: "I didn't go to seminary."

Question: "Where did you go to school?"

Answer: "I went to medical school and became a doctor."

Question: "How did you get into the ministry?"

Answer: "God called me. I put a note on my office door that said 'I have gone to save men's souls.' "

Question: "Did you enter seminary then?"

Answer: "No, I never went to seminary. I simply started preaching. I would read a verse and comment on it. Then read the next verse and comment on it. That's all I've ever done."

The interview with this remarkable man went on for pages,

surveying his whole career in the ministry. The next to the last question was: "Have you learned anything new in your study of the Bible in the last five years?"

"Oh yes," he responded. "Five years ago I began an intensive study of Bible prophecy, and it has led me to the conclusion that we are living in the season of the Lord's return."

My chest tightened with anticipation as I looked to the last question. God was about to speak to me.

Question: "If you were a young minister just beginning to preach, what would your message be?"

Answer: "Flee from the wrath that is to come!"

I could hardly believe my eyes. Those were the exact words God had laid on my heart.

"Thank you, Lord!" I yelled. "Thank you. Thank you. Thank you!"

I was on my knees praising God in prayer. The call had been confirmed in my heart. I was no longer full of doubt. The fear was gone. Resolve had replaced it. I knew what I had to do, and I was ready to do it, regardless — regardless of finances or reputation.

As I drove to the office I found myself slapping the steering wheel in glee one moment, shouting, "Thank you, Lord!" Then in the next moment I would shake my head in astonishment and ask, "But why me Lord? I'm nothing but a miserable sinner."

I've asked the Lord that question many times since, and He has responded graciously in two ways. First, by reminding me that "there is no condemnation for those who are in Christ Jesus" (Rom. 8:1). And second, by reminding me of my namesake, King David of Israel. The Lord has made it clear to me that the only people He has to work through are sinners. He has forgiven and forgotten (Heb. 8:12). He calls us to do the same.

When I arrived at the university, I went directly to the president's office and told him I had decided to resign. He asked what I was upset about. I told him that was not the problem and explained that I was resigning because God had called me to preach. Having been a preacher once himself, the president knew there was no hope in trying to argue with someone who had received God's call.

So, he simply asked, "What church?"

"No church," I replied.

"Well then," he asked, "how are you going to preach?"

"I'm just going to step out in faith and preach wherever God opens a door."

"What are you going to preach?"

"Jesus is coming soon."

He looked at me in disbelief. "You're going to preach what?" he asked.

"That Jesus is coming soon."

He just shook his head in amazement, smiled and said, "When are you going to do this?"

It was the middle of March. I had decided to give him two week's notice.

"April the first," I answered.

He sat there for a moment and stared at me incredulously. Then he shrugged his shoulders and replied, "All I can say is that I think you have selected a most appropriate date!"

So, on April Fool's Day, 1980, I stepped out in faith. Twenty years of running from the Lord was finally over. At long last, with great timidity and only after prolonged discipline, I had said, "Here am I, Lord, send me."

Now I had to learn how to trust the Lord for everything in my life.

Part II:

The Ministry

"There's Never a Dull Moment Serving the Lord"

1) Walking by Faith

The fear that had filled my life for 20 years regarding the Lord's call had dissipated completely when I finally surrendered to the Lord. But during the two weeks between that surrender and the termination of my employment at the university, Satan attacked me hard. I was once again filled with self-doubt. Had I made a rash decision? Was I needlessly jeopardizing my family? Would those who had made pledges be faithful to them? Would any church invite me to speak?

Once I made the decision to resign, the two fears that bothered me most related to my wife and money. How would my wife react? How would I ever pay that business debt? God in His grace and mercy quickly dealt with both fears.

The Lord had blessed me with a beautiful, red-headed wife named Ann who had a disposition exactly opposite to the red headed stereotype. Instead of being moody and volatile, she was stable and quiet — the perfect balance to me! We had grown up together in the same church in Waco, Texas and had been childhood sweethearts.

Ann had always been my number-one fan. I thrived on her support and encouragement. But she had withdrawn that sup-

37

port when I accepted the pulpit in Irving. "I didn't marry a preacher," she announced coldly and, with that proclamation, she withdrew into her own world of public school teaching. She was determined that no one would ever force her into playing the role of a preacher's wife.

Trying to minister without the support of your wife is impossible. The lack of that support had been just one more of the many reasons that my ministry at the church in Irving had failed so miserably.

I could tell that Ann was relieved when I left the ministry and returned to higher education. I therefore greatly feared her reaction when the Lord called me to step out in faith and start preaching again.

My fears proved to be misplaced. When I broke the news to Ann, I discovered that God had already miraculously prepared her heart for my decision. To my astonishment she reacted with enthusiasm, and I took her reaction as one more confirmation of the Lord's call.

One year to the day after the ministry was launched, I returned to Dallas from a pilgrimage to the Holy Land. When Ann met me at the airport, she handed me a present wrapped in paper that said, "Happy Anniversary." I was puzzled.

"It's not our anniversary," I said.

"I know," she replied, "but today is a very special anniversary for both of us."

With those words it suddenly dawned on me that it was the first anniversary of the ministry — April 1, 1981. I opened the package and found a framed certificate that my wife had personally designed. A friend had done the calligraphy. It had the logo of the ministry at the top. Then, in beautiful lettering, it said, "Presented to my husband, David Reagan, on the occasion of the first anniversary of our ministry."

At the bottom was a quotation from I Corinthians 4:10 — "We are fools for Christ's sake."

That plaque is my most prized possession. Everytime I look at it I am reminded of God's grace and mercy and His miracle working ability to transform a human heart.

My second most pressing fear was the business debt. I still had two years of payments to go. Where would the money come from? Again, God in His mercy moved swiftly to remove this mountain from my life. The really neat thing is that He took care of the debt in a way that helped me to better understand the meaning of His grace. I needed that lesson because I was still carrying a lot of legalistic baggage from my religious heritage and my family upbringing.

Part of my view of God had been determined by my relationship with my dad. I suppose this is true to some degree in every person's life. The Bible reveals God as our Heavenly Father. Because of this imagery, it is only natural for a child's view of the Heavenly Father to be shaped by his relationship with his earthly father.

My dad was a strict disciplinarian. He gave little tolerance for misbehavior. He was fast with a belt. I admired him greatly and wanted to please him more than anything, but I always seemed to fall short. And I feared that belt.

I communicated that fear very effectively to my first grade teacher. At the end of the very first week of school she told me I would have to stay after class for talking too much. She lined up the rest of the kids and started marching them down the hall to send them home.

When she got all the way down at the other end of the hall, she suddenly heard me start screaming, "He's going to kill me! He's going to kill me!" She thought someone was in the room trying to hurt me. She ran back and found me alone. I was hysterical. I kept shouting the same thing over and over.

When she finally calmed me down, I explained that my dad was going to "beat me half to death" for having to stay after school. She told me to run home as fast as I could.

Years later when I was 11 years old, I started working for my dad in the summers. He had just opened a sheet metal shop, the first of many successful businesses that he would eventually own. I showed up for work that first day full of enthusiasm. He told me to sweep out the shop. I knew he was a stern taskmaster, so I gave this menial task everything I had. I swept every nook and cranny.

I was just finishing up an outstanding job and was about to sweep the last pile of dust out the back door when my dad walked up.

"What are you doing?" he asked in a gruff sort of way that startled me.

"I'm sweeping out the last pile of dirt," I said, wondering what I could possibly be doing wrong.

He pointed to the floor. "Do you see that rivet?" he asked.

I looked down and saw the glint of a shining rivet through the dust. "Yes sir, I see it."

"Well, pick it up! That rivet cost me a quarter of a cent." He then proceeded with a lecture on the value of a dollar. I needed to know the value of a dollar. But I also needed a word of encouragement about the job I had done.

I stood in awe of my dad, fearful of crossing him in any way, and I projected that relationship onto my Heavenly Father. I felt I could never please God no matter how hard I tried. I had no concept of the meaning of grace.

As the years passed I came to a theological understanding of grace, but it was intellectual rather than experiential, and it therefore did not penetrate my soul. God knew I needed to better understand what grace was all about, and He knew that my fear of my dad stood in the way.

So God touched me with His grace through my dad. Here's how He did it. My dad had used his outstanding credit rating to secure all the loans for the business I had started. But the banks had required my dad to personally guarantee the loans.

That meant that when the business failed my dad's credit was on the line. I was really anxious about what my dad might say or do. I kept waiting for him to read me the riot act. But never once did he speak a harsh word. Never once was he judgmental or condemning. Never once did he remind me that he had advised against going into such a business. He stood by me and encouraged me.

But what would he do now that I was stepping out in faith to serve God? Would he panic over the remaining balance of nearly $25,000? Would he demand that I get a safe job that would ensure the continuance of my monthly payments to the bank?

Again, he said nothing. He remained silent about the matter until about six months after the ministry was established. Then he and Mom called one night. "Son," he said, "your Mom and I have been giving a lot of thought to our finances. We want to get out of debt, so we've decided to consolidate our assets and pay off all our debts. We want you to know that we just paid off the remaining $20,000 that you owe on the business debt."

The mountain was gone—just like that! No more worry about debt. One more fear defeated. Most important of all, my relationship with my dad had been transformed. He had reached out to me in love and given me an incredible blessing I did not deserve and could not repay. Grace experienced. How sweet it is.

Over the next few years I was to learn a lot more about walking by faith, and I am still learning today. One of the first things I learned is that God does not call you to serve Him without spiritually gifting you to fulfill the task He sets before you. You don't have to worry about whether you are qualified to do God's will. If it is God's will that you are doing, He will qualify you.

I discovered, for example, that all my graduate training in international politics had been a perfect preparation for me to teach Bible prophecy. After all, most end-time prophecy is concerned with world politics. That brought a smile to my heart, for I realized that all the time I was running from the Lord, He was preparing me to serve Him when I got tired of running! What is it the Psalm says? — "Even the wrath and rebellion of man goes to the glory of God" (Psalm 76:10). Jonah found that out the hard way, and so did I.

Another discovery I was to make is that God does not put a call on someone without preparing the way for them. When I took the step of faith, I literally had no idea where I would preach. I had broken with the denomination I had grown up in, and there was no way to mend the fences. The church of my heritage was militantly amillennial, even to the point of making the doctrine a test of fellowship. My studies had brought me to a premillennial position.

I had not become identified with any other denomination, so there was no particular group of churches biting at the bit to invite me to speak. Furthermore, the Lord had impressed upon my heart that the new ministry was to be trans-denominational in nature. We were not to identify with any denominational group. We were to go wherever God opened a door, regardless of the sign over that door.

Accordingly, the board of the ministry was composed of people drawn from a great variety of denominations. They agreed on only three things: 1) That Jesus is Lord; 2) That the Bible is the revealed Word of God; and 3) That Jesus is coming soon. Through the power of the Holy Spirit, they put all their differences aside and worked together in love to spread the message of the soon return of Jesus.

My first opportunities for ministry came among a group of churches which constituted a small splinter segment of the church I had been raised in. These churches were anxious to have me speak because their distinctive feature was their premillennial outlook.

They considered me a convert to their cause, and I was invited to make their circuit of churches. But most of them soon lost interest in me when it became obvious that I had no intention of affiliating the ministry with them.

My ministry among these churches lasted for about two years. During that time I learned another lesson about the faith walk. God does not zap anyone with instant spiritual maturity. Growth in the Lord comes through hours of Bible study and prayer, fellowship with the saints and obedient service in the Kingdom.

For two years I preached my heart out to small churches all over this country, most of them with only 40 to 90 members. I had a burning message in my heart that I yearned to share with millions, but I spoke only to dozens, and I began to wonder if the Lord would ever open a door for ministry to greater numbers.

As I look back on those years now, I see that God used them to fine tune my message and to develop me. I had to show my faithfulness in small things before I could be trusted with greater responsibilities. The world calls it "paying your dues." I considered it a time of refinement in the image of Christ. God was shaping me and my message.

My patience was rewarded the third year of the ministry when the Lord prompted the minister of a large church in Lexington, Kentucky to attend a prophecy conference I was conducting at a high school auditorium there. His presence led to an invitation to conduct a prophecy meeting at his church. God greatly blessed that meeting, and the reports of its success led to an avalanche of invitations from a great variety of churches all over the nation.

I'll never forget that meeting. The host pastor had a great sense of humor. When I arrived, we had a conference about the meeting. I didn't know him well, and I did not know his congregation at all.

"What kind of prophecy meeting do you want me to conduct?" I asked.

"What do you mean?" he replied.

"Well," I explained, "I need to know if you want me to jump into the depths of Revelation, or do you want me to deal with prophetic fundamentals?"

He thought for a moment, and then he said, "Dave, when I got married, my wife told me to go to the store and buy her a cookbook. I asked her what kind, and she said, 'Find one that says, Number One: Stand facing the stove.' That's what we need here in the realm of prophecy. Assume we know nothing."

I proceeded on that assumption, and God poured out His Spirit.

In the years since, the Lord has continued to open a great variety of doors to an ever expanding audience. I have spoken to all kinds of churches — Charismatic and non-Charismatic, traditional and renewal, orthodox and unorthodox, dead and alive. You name it. I've been there.

A classic example of the variety is what happened to me one weekend in Abilene, Texas. I was invited to teach a Saturday afternoon prophetic seminar to a Full Gospel Businessmen's convention. After the session, as I was driving out of the parking lot, a man flagged me down. He asked if I had a place to speak the next morning. I said no. He asked if I could stay overnight. I said yes. He then invited me to speak to his Baptist Church at 9 a.m. the next day.

I went back into the motel where the Full Gospel convention was being held. As I was registering for a room to stay overnight, another man walked up and asked if I had a place to speak the next morning. I said yes. He asked what time. I told him. He then invited me to speak at his church at 11 a.m. His church was one of the largest Churches of Christ in the city. I could hardly believe it. Speaking at both a Baptist Church and Church of Christ on the same Sunday morning!

Another thing you learn in a faith walk is that God has a great sense of humor.

So I spoke on Sunday morning at a Baptist Church and a Church of Christ. I drove back to Dallas that day and spoke that evening at an independent Christian Church. On the following Friday evening I preached at one of the largest Episcopal Churches in Dallas.

When the ministry started, I had no idea where I would preach. I still have no idea what door God will open next. But there has never been a lack of doors. I now receive invitations to hold meetings four and five years into the future. I appreciate such invitations but I turn them all down. I figure that a fellow who is preaching the soon return of Jesus has no business making appointments two to five years in the future. So, I take it one year at a time.

2) Receiving Blessings

Preparing, gifting, opening — all of these are essential parts of the faith walk. Another is providing. I learned that God provides all our needs as we lean on Him in faith — not all our desires or wishes or delights, but all our true needs.

The first need I had was a name for the ministry. I searched the Scriptures and called out to God in prayer. One day as I was driving along the highway praying about the matter I felt led to use the name Maranatha Ministries. The ministry had been called to proclaim the soon return of Jesus, and Maranatha is an Aramaic expression that means "Our Lord come!" (II Cor. 16:22). It seemed to be the perfect name.

I was disappointed to find out several weeks later that someone else in Texas had already secured that name. It turned out to be a group in McKinney, a town just north of Dallas. The group was headed up by an optometrist who several years later became a member of our Board. Shortly after that, his Maranatha Ministry contributed five acres of land to our ministry for us to use as a headquarters site. God truly works in strange ways!

When the Maranatha name was turned down, I earnestly began to seek the Lord for another name. Time was short. We needed to get incorporated and apply for tax-exempt status. We needed to print letterheads and brochures. We could do none of those things without a name.

The Lord quickly responded with a new name — Lamb and Lion Ministries. I got excited when He impressed that name upon my spirit. It was perfect. Our message was a prophetic one, and the two great prophetic images of Jesus in the Bible are the suffering lamb and the conquering lion. He has already come as the lamb. He will return as the lion. There was great rejoicing when the Secretary of State of Texas confirmed that we could use the name.

My next need was a logo. I wanted something that would boldly express the ministry's nature and purpose. I had been attracted to the artwork of an illustrator for one of the largest Christian book publishers in America. I found out who he was and discovered that he lived in Austin, Texas. I wrote him a letter describing what I needed and explained that the ministry was new and had no money. In other words, I was boldly asking one of the finest religious artists in the country to draw me a logo free of charge!

I laid my hand on that letter and prayed that God would prepare the man's heart to receive my request. That was the first time I had ever prayed over a letter. It was to be the first of many times.

I waited anxiously for a reply. A month passed. No word. I needed to print letterheads. I was about to give up and go ahead with the printing without a logo when I received a packet in the mail. Inside was a drawing of the perfect logo, better than anything I could ever have hoped for.

God had heard my prayer. He had prepared the way for my letter. The artist's heart had been touched by my plea through the preparation of God's Spirit. The ministry now had an identity—all free of charge. When God does something, He does it first class.

My greatest need was money. We had no cash reserves. No equipment. Not even an office. All we had were pledges totaling $800 per month and Bernice's car, which was almost beyond the pale of prayer! The Board put me on a salary of $1,000 per month, with a housing allowance of $500. With my wife's income as a first-grade teacher, we could get by financially, assuming, of course, that my $1,500 would materialize somehow each month.

I had no idea where my salary would come from. Neither did anyone else except, of course, the Lord. He graciously supplied our needs each month, often in strange and miraculous ways. We would get right to the end of a month, need $700 to pay our bills, and then receive a check for exactly that amount from someone we had never heard of. It was an exciting way to live. The Lord never supplied more than we needed. We ended each month with all our bills paid. We began the next month broke. It kept us on our knees reaching out to God.

One of my most memorable experiences regarding money occurred at a church in central Indiana. Our financial rule for meetings was to go on faith, believing that the Lord would supply our needs through free will love offerings. We had no fees.

On the second night of this particular meeting the pastor asked to speak with me privately. He explained that he and the elders had gotten into an argument about how to compensate me for the meeting. They all agreed that the church should cover my expenses. They disagreed over how to provide a financial gift to the ministry.

"I proposed that they pay you $100 per day or a total of $500 above expenses," the minister explained. "But they said they never heard of paying a preacher that much. They proposed a gift of $300."

I assured the minister that whatever they decided would be fine with me. I reminded him that I had come in faith, believing God would supply our needs.

"I know," he said, "but I want to be fair. What we've decided to do is guarantee the ministry $400. We're going to take up a love offering on the last night of the meeting. However much it falls short of $400, we will make up the difference."

I assured him that would be fine. The next morning I called my office. It was the next to the last day of the month.

"How are we doing financially?" I asked.

"Not so hot," my office manager replied. "We need a total of $1,700 to end the month with all our bills paid. Will your meeting produce that much?"

I told him we could expect only $400 from the meeting. I asked him to get the staff together and have a special prayer session in behalf of the $1,700 we needed. I also got on my knees and started praying the same prayer.

That night a love offering was taken at the end of the service. After the service was dismissed, I went to the door to shake hands with people. I noticed that while I was saying my good-byes to the congregation, the chairman of the board of elders began scurrying around the sanctuary gathering the elders for a special impromptu meeting down front. "Oh no," I thought, "the contribution has fallen far short of $400, and they are reconsidering their commitment to make up the difference."

When the meeting ended, the chairman walked up to me. He stuck out a trembling hand and said, "Dave, we've never had anything happen like this before in the history of this church." In his hand was a check. I opened it and nearly fainted. It totaled $1,725!

I praised God all the way back to my motel. Then I called my office manager at his home, got him out of bed and delivered the good news.

"You'd better total up those bills again," I told him. "You said we owed $1,700. We received $1,725. You know God never gives us one dime more than we need. You missed a $25 bill someplace." And sure enough, he had.

3) Relying on Prayer

I learned quickly that the key to the faith walk is prayer. Earnest prayer. Daily prayer. Specific prayer.

The ministry was only six months old when one of the trustees came to me and said, "Dave, you are killing yourself. You're working night and day, doing everything yourself. You need an office manager."

In full agreement, I explained that there was nothing I could do about it. We just didn't have the money to pay the salary of an office manager.

"The need is there. God knows it and God will supply," the trustee observed. "All you have to do is step out in faith."

But I couldn't take the step. My terrible experience with the business debt had made me overly cautious regarding money. I was paralyzed by the fear of debt and wanted the money in the bank before hiring the much-needed employee.

The trustee was persistent. Every week for a month he either called or came by the office to impress upon me the need for an office manager. He began to wear me down. Then one day shortly before Christmas, he stopped by and dropped a bomb on me.

"Dave, I've been praying daily about your need for an office manager, and God has impressed upon me that I should resign my job and go to work for the ministry. I'm going to do that immediately. I'll report to work on the first Monday in January," he announced.

"But Billy Jack," I protested, "I can't take that risk! How will I ever pay you?"

"You're not the one taking the risk," he wryly observed. "God will supply. Join with me and pray that God will meet the need."

We prayed together. God supplied. At the end of the first month, the money was there. Our monthly income had mysteriously increased just enough to cover his salary.

The Bible says we do not have because we do not ask (James 4:2). I've learned to ask and to ask in faith, believing God will hear and respond.

It took me only two or three meetings to realize that prayer is the key to a successful revival. If the meeting is bathed in prayer beforehand, mighty things will happen, regardless of the quality of my preaching. Souls will be saved. Lives will be transformed. If the people do not pray, as is often the case, nothing will happen. I can preach my heart out, and still nothing will happen.

One of my most dramatic experiences with prayer occurred at a dead meeting I conducted in South Texas.

The church was packed out on Sunday morning, with almost 400 present. There was little response to the invitation that morning. Although that was unusual, it didn't concern me too much because it was a traditional church, and it often took two or three sessions of a meeting in such a church before people would finally loosen up enough to come forward for prayer.

But when the service began on Sunday evening, I knew we were in trouble. There were hardly 100 people present. In four years of ministry I had never seen such a dramatic drop off in attendance between Sunday morning and evening. The apathy was so thick you 1could feel it. I gave the sermon everything I had that night and nothing happened. People just stood there during the invitation and stared blankly. It was a real downer.

On Monday I began to pray earnestly for a spiritual breakthrough. But again, the crowd was small, the singing was listless and the interest was minimal. However, this time during the invitation, the Spirit began to move. I could see people coming under conviction. Some wept. Others hung their heads. Some grabbed the pew in front of them and visibly shook. But they wouldn't move forward. Their feet were in concrete.

We were involved in intense spiritual warfare. The key to victory was prayer. The next day I went to my knees again and cried out to God for a breakthrough. It didn't come. On Tuesday night the Spirit moved with power again. But once more there was a greater level of resistance. People were bleeding to death inside, but they would not come for ministry.

Wednesday was the last day of the meeting. I was wrung out from the intensity of the spiritual battle. Having prayed with zeal for the meeting, now I was the one who needed prayer.

I tried to pray, but the words wouldn't come. I decided to take a drive in the country. As I was driving out of the town, I saw a gaudy temporary sign on the side of the road with a big red arrow on it that pointed to a small building. The sign said, "Do You Need Prayer? If So, Come In!"

I drove on past, but I couldn't get the sign out of my mind. I needed prayer. Why hadn't I stopped? "Probably some shyster after money," I thought. I continued to rationalize my refusal to stop. The rationalizations didn't work. I felt compelled to go back and check out the place.

I knocked tentatively on the door, wondering if I would be greeted by a gypsy with a crystal ball. The Lord had a surprise in store for me. The door was opened by a classic "little old lady in tennis shoes." A sweet smiling, delicately built, elderly lady greeted me. She had the radiance of the Lord all over her.

"Come in," she said, "I've been waiting on you."

Waiting on me? What did she mean by that? I looked around the room. All that was in it were two rocking chairs and a small table. Cookies and coffee were on the table.

She pointed to one of the rocking chairs and asked me to have a seat. She then pulled her chair right up to me, leaned forward and said, "What can we pray about?"

Still suspicious, I asked, "Do you charge?"

"Oh Heavens no!" she replied, with a hearty laugh. "I serve the living God, and He doesn't charge for His grace and mercy. Now, what do you want to pray about?"

"Well, first of all," I said, "tell me what you're doing here."

She patiently explained that God had spoken to her heart six months before and told her to come to this town and open a roadside prayer chapel.

"This town needs revival," she said.

I could sure agree with that! Again, she pressed me for my prayer request. But I had one more question for her.

"What did you mean when you said, 'I've been expecting you?'"

She smiled. "You probably won't believe this," she said hesitantly, "but God spoke to my heart yesterday afternoon while I was praying. He told me a preacher would come by this morning for special prayer. You are a preacher, aren't you?"

I was speechless. How did she know I was a preacher? I was driving an old beat up pickup truck that I had borrowed. And I was dressed in a flannel shirt with jeans. I sure didn't look like a preacher.

"Yes," I replied, "I'm a preacher."

"I thought so," she said. "The Lord told me you were coming. I got here early this morning, swept out the place and made this coffee and cookies for you. Where have you been? I've been waiting for two hours!"

I began to praise God for his grace and mercy. We joined hands and praised Him together. She prayed in tongues while I just kept repeating "Thank you, Lord. Thank you, Lord."

I described my plight to her in detail. She kept nodding her head knowingly.

"I understand what you're up against," she said. "That's why God sent me here. This town desperately needs revival."

She then began to pray for a Holy Ghost blow-out at the church that evening. I thought she was going to pray Heaven down. Never had I experienced such boldness and power in prayer.

That night she came and sat on the back row and continued to pray silently all through the service. I could feel the power when I preached. I could sense the spiritual tension in the congregation building to a climax.

The dam broke when the invitation was offered. People came flooding to the front with tears streaming down their faces. Some dropped to their knees in repentance. Others hugged each other and offered words of encouragement. It was a beautiful spiritual scene. God had given the victory through prayer.

Another discovery I've made about prayer is that it is the key to pacing the faith walk. This is one of the most difficult lessons for any Christian to learn, particularly for those who are called into the full-time ministry.

If we are going to walk in faith, we must walk at God's pace, not ours. That's tough. Most of us tend to lag behind. The Lord has to drag us screaming and kicking every step of the way.

For ministers, the problem is usually just the opposite. We tend to run ahead of the Lord. Like Abraham when he sired Ishmael, we try to help the Lord out. We get enthusiastic about what we are doing, we get impatient with the Lord's pace and we start running ahead of the Lord. That always means big trouble.

I'm convinced that many of the ministries that are suffering severe debt today are in that condition primarily because they are not moving at God's intended pace for them. Our God owns the cattle on a thousand hills. He can supply every need. When we run ahead, He leaves the needs for us to meet. The result, too often, is desperate fund appeals that do not bring any honor to the name of Jesus.

God wants us to walk at the pace He desires. To do that, it is essential that we spend a lot of time on our knees seeking His will on every decision.

4) Believing in Miracles

A serious prayer life leads inevitably to a belief in miracles. I have discovered that most Christians do not pray very frequently. It is not surprising, therefore, that most Christians have rejected the miraculous.

Many have been victimized, like I was, by the ultradispensational teaching that the age of miracles ceased at the end of the First Century. Another problem is that many Christians have almost defined miracles out of existence by stating that a miracle must violate a law of nature.

The Bible says God is the same yesterday, today and forever. He does not change. He is still a personal, caring and miracle-working God. He created the physical laws of the universe, and

He can suspend them anytime He pleases. Unlike the moral laws, the physical laws are not inviolate.

But what most people overlook is the fact that there are very few miracles in the Bible that violate any law of nature. Most Biblical miracles are of a different sort. They are miracles of timing. Hannah prays for her womb to be blessed and it is. There was no immaculate conception. She had a husband. Her pregnancy was a miracle of timing.

Likewise, Paul and Silas were released from jail by an earthquake. No laws of nature were violated. Earthquakes are very common in Israel. But isn't it interesting that this particular earthquake occurred at the moment Paul and Silas were praying for deliverance — and it occurred in just the right place! It reminds me of another earthquake that served Joshua and the Children of Israel at Jericho.

Or consider Elijah who prayed that it would not rain in Israel. It did not rain for three and half years, not until he prayed again for the rain to come. Did that miracle violate any law of nature? There is no law of nature that says it must rain in Israel every year. Israel often experiences severe droughts. The miracle was one of timing. The rain stopped and started in sequence with the prayers. The world calls it "coincidence." I call it "God-incidence."

I personally experienced one of these God-incidences when I went to Lexington, Kentucky to hold a meeting at a large church with several thousand members. The church had taken seriously a call to prayer I had sent them in a letter. They had conducted special prayer services. Some had committed themselves to both prayer and fasting. Over 100 had volunteered to conduct an all night prayer vigil, with a different person coming to the church to pray every 10 minutes for a 24-hour period.

When I was informed about all this prayer activity, I got excited. I knew God would greatly bless their prayers with a mighty move of His Spirit.

I arrived for the meeting two days early because I had some other business to tend to in Lexington. I had hardly checked into my motel room on Friday morning when I was suddenly struck by an extremely sharp pain in the groin area. The pain was absolutely excruciating. I laid down on the bed hoping it would go away.

It didn't. It intensified.

I called a taxi and went to the emergency room of the nearest hospital. Several hours later, after many tests and X-rays, the doctor informed me that I had a kidney stone that had lodged in my ureter. He told me that I should be admitted to the hospital immediately for treatment, including possible surgery.

Despite the pain, all I could think about was the wonderful meeting I knew God had prepared for me through the prayers of the congregation. I knew we were in store for a spiritual feast, and I didn't want to miss it. So, I refused admission to the hospital. The doctor told me I was crazy. He explained that if the stone started moving, I would experience even worse pain. I still refused admission. He then gave me some powerful pain-killing pills and warned me that they might knock me out completely. So he urged caution in taking them.

I went back to the motel still racked with pain. I threw the pills away, convinced that this was a spiritual battle. I believed with all my heart that Satan had come against me with the express purpose of keeping me from preaching. He knew the congregation was on the verge of a great revival, and he was determined to stop it. I was equally determined to stand against him.

I stopped praying for healing. I started praying instead for spiritual strength to stand against Satan. I rebuked him and called upon the name of Jesus for victory.

The pain persisted. I tossed and tumbled all night long, hoping I would awake to find the pain gone. It wasn't. About noon I got an idea. I picked up the phone and called a dear friend, one of the godliest persons I knew in Lexington. He had been born on the mission field in China and had later become a missionary to the Philippines. He was a man of prayer, and that's what I needed.

He agreed to come right away. He brought a friend with him.

The three of us sat in my room and talked for about 30 minutes. Then, he laid his hands on me and prayed a simple, quiet prayer: "Lord, dissolve the kidney stone so that David can fulfill your purposes in the meeting that starts tomorrow. In Jesus' name, Amen." That's all he said. No fanfare. No theatrics.

We talked for another 20 to 30 minutes and then they stood up to leave. When I arose, the pain instantly left. I knew the Lord had dissolved the stone. Satan had been defeated. We rejoiced in thanksgiving to the Lord.

The next morning I shared the miracle of my healing with the church. They responded with enthusiastic applause that startled even me. It was a remarkable beginning to what proved to be one of the most Spirit anointed meetings I have ever held.

A week later when I returned to Dallas I shared the story with a friend who is a radiologist. He was skeptical. "Maybe God did heal you," he said, "but we need to check it out." He put me through another battery of tests and X-rays, but he could not find a trace of the stone. Of course not, God had dissolved it!

One of the most dramatic miracles I have witnessed in my ministry occurred at a home worship service in north Dallas. About 25 people had gathered for an evening of devotional praise. Right before the service was to start, I was standing near the front door when I heard the door bell ring. I opened the door and there stood an old friend I had not seen for a long time. I stuck out my hand to shake hands with her, but she quickly drew her hand back.

"What's wrong?" I asked.

"Take a look at my hand," she replied.

She thrust her right hand toward me. On the top of her hand was an ugly, red blister, about the size of a silver dollar.

"I just burned my hand severely with some grease," she explained. "I heard about this worship service over the grapevine and decided to come. Then, right before I left the house, I spilled grease on my hand. I almost didn't come."

I offered my sympathy for her badly burned hand. By then the worship service was starting, so we hurried to the living room.

All we did that evening was lift up the Lord in praise. But I have discovered that there is great power in praise. When we lose ourselves in love and adoration for the Lord, we open ourselves to His ministry. The Psalms say that "God inhabits the praises of His people" (Psalm 22:3).

The Lord's Spirit came that evening and was enthroned upon our praises. It was a service of quiet and reverent praise and worship. When the service ended, my friend came up to me with tears running down her cheeks. She was on the verge of breaking into sobs.

"What's the matter"" I asked. "Is your hand hurting a lot?"

"Oh no," she said, "that's why I'm so upset. Look what the Lord has done."

Once again she held out her hand. The blister was gone. There was no redness. The hand was perfectly normal. I could hardly believe my eyes.

"When did that happen?" I asked.

"I don't know," she replied. "I have no idea except that it happened sometime during the praise service."

No one had prayed specifically for her. No one had laid hands on her or anointed her with oil. She had simply lifted her hands in praise to God, and the Lord had responded by touching her with His healing hand.

The Bible speaks of gifts of healing — in the plural (I Cor. 12:9). God gave me one of those gifts shortly after I began the ministry.

I was holding a meeting for a tiny church of only 30 souls. The church met in a shopping center in southeast Dallas. On the last night of the meeting I preached on "The Power of God." The purpose of the sermon was to convince people that God is personal and loving, that He hears prayers and answers them, and that He still performs miracles.

I used many Biblical examples to illustrate my points. One of the examples was the story of Hannah and how God blessed her barren womb. That story had always had a special place in my heart.

When I offered the time of personal ministry, the worship leader suddenly signaled for another man to come up and take his place. Then he motioned to his wife to come join him at the front. The two of them came up to me and asked me to pray that God would enable them to have a child. They explained that they had one girl about seven years old who suffered brain damage at birth and could not walk or talk. They said they had been trying to have another child ever since the first one had been born, but the doctors had told them they would not be able to have any more children.

I looked them right in the eye and asked, "Do you believe that with God all things are possible?"

"Oh yes!" they replied in unison.

I laid hands on them and prayed that God would bless her womb.

Three months later the husband called me at the office. "You're not going to believe this," he shouted, "but my wife is pregnant!" He then began shouting, "Praise the Lord! Praise the Lord!" I joined him, and we had a Holy Spirit pep rally right there over the phone.

Three months later he called again. This time he was more subdued. His voice sounded almost awe-struck. "Dave, that was some prayer you prayed over us. Guess what? We're going to have twins!"

They did. Two boys, named Jonathan and James. They are now four years old. I have a picture of them hanging on my office wall as a constant reminder of God's love and mercy and power.

Three years after the boys were born, their sister died in her sleep. She was only 10 years old. When I heard the news, I immediately understood why God had blessed that family with twins. He knew all along that He was about to call that little girl home. So He gave them two.

In the years since, I have prayed for hundreds of barren wombs, and I have a drawer full of photographs of babies born to women who had been declared "incurably barren."

One incident I will never forget occurred in a town in Oklahoma.

I was holding a meeting at an independent church. One of the members of that church was the leading obstetrician in town. He called me one day at the motel where I was staying and told me that he wanted me to pray with a patient of his. "I've done everything I can for her," he explained. "It's up to God." He said she would get in touch with me.

About an hour later I received a phone call from a man who identified himself as the pastor of one of the largest Baptist Churches in the town. He asked if we could get together for a get-acquainted chat. I agreed and offered to meet him at his office because the church was located right next to the motel.

"Oh no!" he said, "I don't think it would be wise for you to come here. I'll come to your room."

In a few minutes he was at my door. We sat and talked for over an hour. Our conversation ranged over a great variety of topics — church growth, evangelism, spiritual gifts and, finally, healing. All the time I was wondering about the purpose of his visit. The topic of healing finally brought him to the point of his visit.

"Let me tell you the main reason I came over here," he said. "My wife desperately wants to have a second child, but the doctors don't think it's possible. Her physician suggested to her this morning that she let you pray for her. I wanted to check you out first to make sure you weren't some sort of looney faith healer. I've decided I'd like for you to pray for her."

I appreciated his concern for his wife and his desire to prevent her from being hurt further by some emotional and manipulative "faith healer." I rejoiced that I had passed the "looney" test!

He called her. She came over to the room. We sat in a circle, held hands and prayed. This past Christmas I received a beautiful photograph of that couple holding their new baby.

The greatest miracles God performs today are often taken for granted. They are the internal miracles of the heart. I'm speaking of miracles like the sinner who repents and is delivered from bondage to sin. Or the backslidden Christian whose heart is suddenly transformed from apathy to zeal.

I'll never forget a dramatic moment at a meeting in Indiana where the Spirit of God fell mightily at the invitation time. Many responded to the Lord that morning, but the person who led the way was a woman who grabbed my hand, squeezed it hard, looked directly in my eyes and said, "I have a heart as hard as granite, and I want God to break it."

He did. Today she is a vital member of my ministry's staff, devoting her life to the Lord's service.

The most memorable breaking of a heart by the Holy Spirit that I ever witnessed took place during a meeting in California. It was the last night. When I offered the time of ministry, the Spirit began moving with great power. Many responded. I announced we would sing only one more verse of the invitation song.

As we started that verse, a fellow built like a Mack truck stepped out into the aisle near the back of the sanctuary and started forward. As he advanced toward the front, he gained momentum. He was almost running as he got within a few yards of me. I thought I was going to be run over! Just as he reached me he slammed on the brakes and embraced me with a big bear hug. Then he dropped to the floor in a convulsion of tears. I went to the floor with him.

He was crying and sobbing so hard he could barely speak. As I struggled to get to my feet, I whispered in his ear that I was going to get the elders to pray with him. He grabbed my arm and pulled me back down. "No! No!" he gasped between sobs. "Don't call the elders. I've got to talk to someone who doesn't know me." I helped him over to the podium steps and told him I would be back to pray with him after the service.

He had composed himself by the time I returned.

"What can I pray with you about?" I asked.

He lowered his head and spoke softly. "These folks at this church think I'm a good Christian man," he said, "but I'm full of rottenness. You see, I've been plotting to kill a man for three months. I was going to do it this next week. But God's Word just got hold of my heart tonight, and I know now that I can't go through with it. I want to turn it over to the Lord."

I was stunned. What power there is in God's Word! Two lives were about to be saved as I knelt beside that man, joined hands with him and lifted up his hate-filled heart for God to heal. The deliverance was instantaneous and he went home rejoicing.

5) Leaning on the Spirit

One of the central lessons I had to learn in my faith walk is how to live on God's power rather than my own. It is a constant, never-ending struggle. I desire to lean on the power of God's Spirit, but I find myself continually falling back on self-reliance.

I often feel like Paul in Romans 7 where he said he had a battle going on within him between good and evil. "I desire to do what is right," he wrote, "but I end up doing the very thing I hate" (Rom. 7:15-19). For a long time this internal war really baffled me. I couldn't understand why it was still going on even after I had been born again.

I sought the answer in God's Word, and I found it. I discovered that I am composed of body, soul and spirit (I Thess. 5:23) and that the only part of me that was born again when I accepted Christ was my spirit. My body will not be redeemed until the resurrection (Rom. 8:23). The redemption of my soul — my mind and will and emotions — is a process that began at my spiritual rebirth and will continue until I either die or am raptured. In the Scriptures, that process is called sanctification. It is a process whereby God's Spirit seeks to shape our souls into the image of Jesus (Rom. 8:29 and II Cor. 3:18).

In other words, our salvation is an on-going process. It begins with our justification (the salvation of our spirit), proceeds with sanctification (the salvation of our soul), and is culminated in glorification (the salvation of our body). For the believer, salvation is past, present and future.

This helped me to understand the struggle going on within me. Every time I tried to make a decision, my spirit, which is redeemed and in tune with God's Spirit, would urge me in God's direction. At the same time, my unredeemed soul, still in contact with the world, would pull me in Satan's direction.

The Lord has allowed struggles to come into the ministry from time to time. He has used these to teach me how to rely on Him rather than myself. Sometimes I have succeeded. Sometimes I have failed. But I have learned from all the confrontations that if I will trust in Him and rely on the power of His Spirit, He will deliver me.

My most painful confrontation occurred shortly after the ministry was established. I got a call from a preacher in McKinney, Texas, a town just north of Dallas. He was ministering at a church that represented the heritage I had grown up in. He asked me if I would come over to his church and speak to a group of ministers about Bible prophecy.

I was immediately suspicious. I knew that religious heritage well. I had spent 30 years in it. I knew the preachers were all militantly amillennial in their prophetic viewpoint. I also knew that there was nothing they loved more than to argue. They were in bondage to a spirit of debate.

When I was growing up in that church, debating had been one of our favorite pastimes. We would pick some cocky little banty rooster and turn him loose on some "denominational preacher," and then we would yell for blood. It was anything but a spiritually enriching experience.

I was not about to be drawn into such an ungodly event, so I declined the minister's invitation.

"But why?" he persisted.

"Because I know from experience," I said bluntly, "that you fellows are not interested in learning anything. You just want to argue. You're trying to set me up for a scalping."

"Oh no!" he protested. "You don't understand. This is a regular monthly meeting of all our ministers in the county. We invite someone to read a paper for an hour, then we question them for an hour, and then we all go have lunch together."

I was tempted to accept. The man sounded sincere. But I had too many memories of past experiences. I refused his invitation.

A week later he called again. Again, I refused. Then he came by my office. He kept assuring me that the invitation was on the up and up, that it was not a setup, and that he would take personal responsibility for keeping the meeting orderly. I was impressed by his persistence and his sincerity. With much reservation, I finally agreed to speak.

The moment I arrived at his church I knew I was in trouble. I spotted preachers who had driven in from as far away as 200 miles. Some of them I recognized as notorious "head hunters" — a term we used for self-appointed defenders of the faith who were always looking for a heretic to nail to the wall.

No one spoke to me except the host minister. The tension was thick. I was being glared at from every angle. I decided immediately that I would not mention the word "millennium." That word to this group would be like waving a red flag in front of a bull. They did not believe Jesus would ever put His foot on this earth again — and they were ready to fight to the death to defend that belief. I decided to speak on why I believe Jesus is coming soon for His church. I focused on signs of the times. I never breathed the unspeakable word, "millennium."

As I spoke, some stared blankly at the ceiling, others passed notes to each other, and some even pulled out books and read them! It was obvious they had not come to listen. They had come to sharpen their knives during the question-and-answer period.

When I finished, we took a 10-minute break. Again, no one

spoke to me, but that was fine with me because I spent that 10 minutes praying non-stop that God would enable me to hold my Irish temper and to deal with them in love. By the time the question-and-answer period began, the Lord was in control of me, and I was at peace.

The host minister, who proved to be an honest and sincere man, had sensed the intense spirit of hostility. So, before he opened the meeting to questions, he gave a little speech.

"Gentlemen," he said bravely, "I want to remind you that this man is our guest. We invited him to speak. He did not invite himself. I will expect you to treat him like a guest. Is that understood?"

No one said a word.

"Furthermore, I want to remind you that the next part of our program is a question-and-answer period. All I want are questions. No sermons. And the questions must be on one topic only — Bible prophecy. Is that understood?"

Again, only silence. The host minister then turned to an elderly gentleman and said, "Brother, you are our senior minister, so you get to ask the first question."

The old gentleman, who looked to be over 80, turned to me, glared, and then literally shouted, "I have only one question for you, and it don't have anything to do with prophecy!"

Somehow, instinctively, I knew it was not going to be a friendly question.

"Young man," he sneered with contempt, "I don't care what you have to say about prophecy unless you can answer this question correctly. Do you believe in baptism?"

I had spoken for one hour on the second coming of Jesus, and all this fellow wanted to know was my position on baptism! And he had been told point blank to limit his questions to prophecy.

"Of course I believe in baptism," I responded. "Now, what is your question about prophecy?"

"Wait a minute," he shouted. "You're not going to get off that easy. Let me put the question another way." He thought for a moment, and then he continued. "When you bring a person to Jesus, do you baptize him by immersion for the remission of his sins?"

"Of course I do," I responded again. "Now, what's your question about prophecy?"

By this time the man was almost livid. The trap he had laid for me was not working. He waved his hands in protest.

"Wait a minute," he repeated. "Let me put the question another way. Do you believe that Baptists are saved?"

"Of course," I replied. "Now what's ..." I never got the words out of my mouth.

He jumped to his feet and started screaming, "I thought so! I thought so! You don't believe in baptism! Anyone who believes a Baptist can be saved doesn't believe in baptism!"

While I was trying valiantly to figure out the logic of that statement, the host jumped to his feet, motioned the preacher to sit down, and proceeded to give his speech again. Be nice. This man is our guest. No sermons. Only questions about Bible prophecy. Understood? Silence.

The first person to stick his hand in the air was sitting at the other end of the room. When he was called on, he jumped from his chair, ran to the front and stuck his finger in my face. He too was more than a little livid.

"I want you to know that I also disagree with you," he shouted. "I disagree with everything you said, particularly what you said about the millennium."

I could hardly believe my ears. "But I didn't say anything about the millennium!" I protested.

"You didn't?" He seemed amazed.

"No, I didn't even mention the word. All I said is that Jesus is coming soon. Do you disagree with that?"

"No," he said, "but I disagree with the way you said it!"

The man had obviously not heard a word I had said. Again, the host was on his feet trying to bring order to a hopeless situation. Again, he explained the ground rules.

The next question was, at last, a relevant one. "Why are you so obsessed with the Jews?"

I thanked the Lord for the question and then launched into a lengthy survey of why the Jew is so central to the understanding of Bible prophecy. By the time I finished that question I had new hope that the meeting could be salvaged. My hope went down the drain fast.

The next person recognized stood up, buttoned his coat, straightened his tie, and then very slowly, deliberately and piously made a statement without ever looking at me. "Gentlemen," he said, "my Bible tells me what to do with a man like this. My Bible tells me to mark him and not to eat with him." He turned to me. "I hereby announce that I refuse to eat lunch with you!"

It was the last straw for the host. "I've had enough of this," he snapped. "I will not allow this man to be subjected to this kind of abuse any longer. The meeting is adjourned."

"Wait a minute," I interrupted. "I didn't come here to cause trouble. I came to witness my faith. I don't want to mess up your lunch plans. I'll go home, and all of you can eat together."

"No!" said the host. "You're not going home. I invited you to eat, and I'm going to buy your lunch."

"No you're not!" someone shouted. Everyone turned to see who had spoken. It was a short fat man who had not said a word up to that time. "You're not going to buy Dave's lunch," he explained, "because I'm going to buy it!"

I had found one friend, a man with a lot of courage. After the meeting was adjourned, I went up to this new-found friend, put my arm around his shoulders and said, "Brother, you've got a lot of class."

"On no," he protested. "I don't have any class at all."

"Yes you do," I insisted.

But he continued to protest vehemently, saying, "I've got no class." When I asked him why he was so insistent on that point, he replied, "Because I'm the minister of a non-class church!" We both broke into gales of laughter.

You're probably wondering what we were laughing about. Let me explain. The church of my heritage was so legalistic that it split into more than 25 different groups. They all used the same denominational name, but they wouldn't have anything to do with each other. Since they all used the same name, we had to devise labels to differentiate ourselves. Some were called "Pre-Mills." Others were classified as "Antis." There were the "One Cuppers." And there were the "Non-Class" brethren. These latter folks felt it was wrong to have Sunday School classes. The brother who stood by me that day was the minister of one of these "Non-Class" churches — and that's the reason he was so insistent upon denying that he had any class.

Well, believe it or not, we all went to a restaurant for lunch. Thirty men pulled tables together, sat in a corner and whispered. I sat on the opposite side of the restaurant with the host, the "Non-Class" minister, and a third man who joined us. He turned out to be the minister of an independent Christian Church in the area. When I asked him what he was doing at the meeting, he smiled, put his arm around the "Non-Class" minister and said, "They're trying to convert the two of us!" So, I had lunch with the host and the two outcasts.

The whole experience gave me an idea of how Jesus must have felt when he was confronted by the Scribes and Pharisees.

I soon had another challenging experience with my former religious heritage. Thankfully, it turned out much better.

One of my trustees moved from Dallas to Houston and started attending one of the churches of my heritage. It was a somewhat less traditional church, with more openness and freedom, but it still had a lot of its denomination's hangups.

When people in Houston began to urge that I come down there and conduct a prophecy seminar, I asked trustees in that area to scout out a site for the meeting. The trustee who had recently moved there called and suggested that I conduct the seminar on a Saturday afternoon at his new found church. I reminded him that they did not share my prophetic viewpoint. He said he was going to ask them anyway.

I was astonished when he called back and said they had agreed for me to use the building. Not only that, they had also asked me to speak to their church on Sunday morning.

There were, however, two stipulations. The advertising for the prophecy seminar had to state that it was not endorsed by the church. And with regard to the Sunday morning sermon, I was free to speak on any topic except prophecy. I agreed to both stipulations.

Almost no one from the church was present that Saturday afternoon for the seminar. That didn't surprise me. The next morning I went to the church not knowing what to expect. I tried to prepare myself for the worst — some ugly public confrontation. The Lord had a surprise in store for me.

I arrived in time for Sunday school. One of the elders met me at the door and asked, "Is it true that you have just returned from Israel?" I told him that was right. "Well then," he said, "would you take over our adult class in the auditorium and tell us about Israel?"

I felt a flush of excitement. What an invitation! What an opportunity to talk about my favorite topic. "Let me ask you something," I said cautiously. "Will I be free to say anything I please about Israel?"

"Oh yes!" said the elder. I don't think he had any idea what he was asking for.

I jumped into the presentation with great enthusiasm. I decided to pour it on — to give them a panoramic overview of the Jew in Bible prophecy, from the Abrahamic Covenant to its fulfillment with the primacy of the nation of Israel during the millennial reign of Christ.

I expected to be thrown out at the end. Instead, another elder jumped up and began praising the presentation. "This has been fantastic!" he said. "I didn't know any of these prophecies were even in the Bible. How could we have overlooked them for so long?" I had often asked myself the same question.

At the morning worship service, I was true to my promise. I avoided prophecy. I spoke on faith. At the end of the service, another elder came to the front and expressed his appreciation for both the teaching and the preaching. He then asked if I would be willing to return that evening to speak some more on prophecy! I just couldn't believe what was happening. I said I would be happy to return — and started praising the Lord in my spirit.

Then the elder did something beyond belief. He said he knew the whole congregation had been greatly blessed, so he wanted to give them an opportunity to express their appreciation. "We were going to give this man $100," he said, "but we've been blessed far beyond that, so let's take up a special love offering right now!"

That evening I spoke for an hour on Bible prophecy and then opened it up to questions. The people responded enthusiastically. The questions were sincere and probing. They showed that the people were open and eager to learn.

As I left that evening, one of the deacons called me aside. He put a hand on my shoulder and shook his head in amazement. "Dave," he said, "you're not going to believe what a miracle God has performed here today."

He then told me something that shocked me. He said that one of their elders had been very opposed to my coming and had even spoken out publicly against me, branding me as a "false prophet." He explained that was the reason so few of their members had attended the seminar the day before.

"What I'm telling you," he said, "is that you walked into a very hostile environment. And yet, God turned it around in one day's time! Not only were you invited back this evening, but I have an unbelievable check to give you from this morning's love offering." He handed me the check, hugged me and said, "God bless you, brother."

The check was for $1,500. It was the largest single offering the ministry had ever received up to that time.

I was to be invited back to that church many times to teach and preach on prophecy. The hostile elder eventually left, and the church moved on to a deeper walk with the Lord, ultimately even changing its name to one that was truly non-denominational.

One of the strangest confrontations I've had in the ministry occurred in Ft. Worth, Texas at the office of a denominational administrator. His title was Regional Minister, but he was, in effect, the bishop of 400 churches in Texas and New Mexico. He had sent me a letter asking me to call his secretary and arrange an appointment for a "get-acquainted session."

I suspected that he had more in mind than that, but I didn't know what. I found out fast, as soon as I arrived.

"Have a seat," he said. "I'll be back in a moment. I'm going to get a witness."

"A witness?" I responded in surprise. "What do you need a witness for?"

"Because I'm going to read you the riot act!" he said.

That is exactly what he proceeded to do, once he got his witness in place.

"I want you to get out of my churches and stay out of my churches," he snarled.

"Why do you feel that way?" I asked.

"Because I don't want my people hearing your message about the second coming of Jesus."

"Why not?"

"Because it's a bunch of bunk. Jesus is never coming back! All you're doing is just frightening and confusing people. So stay out of my churches!"

My emotions at that point were very mixed. I was angry. Who did this guy think he was speaking constantly about "his" churches? I was appalled. How could a man responsible for 400 churches be so unbelieving and apostate? I was sad. I kept thinking about all those people sitting in the pews of "his" churches, hungering for the Word of God.

I wanted to jump up and denounce the man as an agent of Satan. I wanted to get on my knees and pray for him. I really didn't know what to do. I just sat there and prayed for the Lord's peace as he continued to rail against me.

"There's another thing about you I don't like," he said. "You're a Salvationist."

That really caught me off guard. I had been called a lot of names in my life, but never a "Salvationist." He had used it as a slur, but it really didn't sound so bad. I was confused.

"What do you mean by that?" I asked.

"You're one of those guys who thinks that a fellow can kneel down in a field while chopping cotton and ask the Lord to come into his life — and thus be saved."

"OK," I responded, "I confess. I'm a 'Salvationist.' What are you?"

I'll never forget his answer. In one sentence he summarized the apostasy of so much of Christendom: "I believe that every person on the face of the earth who is growing more mature is in the process of being saved."

"Does that include Buddhists? Hindus? Atheists?"

"Everyone!" he snapped. "As long as they are growing more mature."

No, he was not a "Salvationist." He was a Universalist masquerading as a Christian. He claimed to follow Jesus, but he was standing there denying the essentiality of the atoning blood of Jesus. Salvation was equated with maturity. The Cross was irrelevant.

As I stood to leave, I noticed a statement framed on his wall. I thought it was a peculiar one for his office. It said, "We speak where the Bible speaks. We are silent where the Bible is silent."

A confrontation of a totally different type took place in New Mexico a few years later. It was a tough one — the type that can easily generate bitterness. The experience impressed upon me again the importance of turning such things over to the Lord.

It all began with a desperate phone call from a distraught

young minister whom I had met only once before. He begged me to come to his church immediately and conduct a revival. He said they were in a terrible condition and needed some encouragement. Their senior pastor had suddenly resigned several months before and had left them with an enormous debt on a new building. Since that time the attendance had dwindled, the contributions had dropped off sharply, all the staff members except him had been released, and the remaining members were about to lose their building to the bank.

It sounded beyond hope to me, but the young man was so earnest and persistent that I decided to go, if at all possible. It was early December when he called. I explained that I was booked solid for meetings during the next year except for the month of January — a month when most churches try to avoid special meetings because of unpredictable weather.

"Any time would be fine," he said. "Just come fast!"

I flew to New Mexico in late January. The young man met me at the airport, and en route to the motel it became painfully obvious that he was on the verge of a full-fledged nervous breakdown. He began to weep as he told me about his plight.

He had been the youth minister. When things started falling apart, all responsibility had been dumped on him. He was currently serving as youth minister, education director, pulpit preacher and janitor! And they had not given him any increase in salary.

The meeting was well attended despite the fact that the congregation had dwindled down to less than 100. I had held five meetings at different churches in that area, and all those churches supported the meeting by bringing vans and buses full of people each evening.

As I do with all my meetings, I had gone there on a faith basis, meaning that I would rely on love offerings to meet my expenses and compensate the ministry. Each evening one of the church's leaders made a plea for an offering, indicating that everything given would be passed on to Lamb and Lion Ministries. This is normal procedure.

The morning I was to fly out, the young preacher, still weeping, drove me to the airport. As I got ready to board the plane, he handed me an envelope.

"Don't open this until you get on the plane," he said. "When you open it, you will understand what I'm up against."

The envelope contained a check for $125. I was horrified. The church, or rather its leaders, had stolen the offering! They had kept it for their building fund. I was handed a token that didn't even cover my expenses.

As I said before, it is easy to get bitter about experiences like this one. As I sat there on that plane, I felt myself getting madder and madder. "Why those guys are nothing but a bunch of crooks," I thought. And then I turned my rage on the Lord. "Lord!" I thought, "why did you let this happen?"

His answer to my heart was short and simple. "I thought you came in faith. If you did, then believe I have it under control. Forgive and move on."

It was hard to do but, by leaning on the power of God's Spirit, I was able to overcome the bitterness and forgive.

And, as usual, God poured out His blessings. The plane I boarded that day was not going back home. It was headed for California where I had a meeting scheduled at a large church in the Los Angeles area. The offerings of the people at that church totaled $6,000 — the largest offering the ministry had ever received.

And, speaking of "God-incidences," I discovered that the distraught young man in New Mexico was a "Timothy" of the church in Los Angeles. He had grown up in that church and had been encouraged by them to become a minister. When they heard about his condition, the leaders of the church arranged for the young man to fly to California immediately. They put him up in an apartment and just let him rest in the Lord for six months before they found him a new ministry position. He was one of their spiritual investments, and they were not about to lose him.

As Jeremiah put it, "The steadfast love of the Lord never

ceases. His mercies never come to an end. They are new every
morning" (Lam. 3:22-23 — RSV).

6) Preaching with Power

Learning to lean on the Lord is always the most difficult in
those areas where you are naturally talented. After all, why do
you need the Lord's help when you have the natural talent to
handle it yourself? Isn't your talent "God-given"? So, when you
rely on your talent, aren't you really relying on God? It is so
easy to rationalize away our unwillingness to yield to God and
operate within His will and by His power.

My greatest natural talent has always been my public speaking
ability. I won more contests than I could keep count of in junior
high, high school and college. I was versatile. I excelled in dra-
matics, declamation, poetry interpretation, debate — just about
anything that required me to open my mouth! When I was a junior in high school, I won first in the State of Texas in oratory. It
was only natural that I should gravitate into a profession like
teaching, where a gift for gab would be a great plus.

When I finally yielded to the Lord's call on my life and began
to preach at the church in Irving, I expected to excel at preaching
without any difficulty whatsoever. A rude shock awaited me.

I quickly discovered that natural talent is not the key to effective service in the Lord's kingdom. No matter how much I
polished my sermons or rehearsed them in front of a mirror,
they just did not seem to have any power. They were often in-
sightful, even eloquent and inspiring, but they were devoid of
spiritual power. It was maddening.

The Lord impressed the problem upon me from time to time
in a very interesting way. Once in a while someone would say to

me, "Oh thank you. You said something in your sermon today that I really needed to hear. I was blessed." When I would ask what it was that I had said, I realized that almost invariably it was something that was not contained in my sermon notes! The blessings from my mouth always seemed to come forth at those infrequent moments when I would let my guard down and venture to say something I had not intended to say. That was puzzling — until I turned to the Word and began an intensive study of spiritual gifts.

I soon discovered that there is a great difference in a gift and a talent. Talents are natural. Gifts are supernatural. The Word teaches that every person who is born again receives at least one spiritual gift at the time of his rebirth (I Cor. 12:4-11). He may receive more than one. If he is a good steward of the gifts he receives, he may even be given additional gifts as his walk with the Lord progresses.

We are often gifted in an area of natural talent, but not always. A person who is a naturally talented singer might be gifted by the Spirit to use that talent for the Lord's glory, but then, again, the person might not be. When they aren't, we usually tend to write off their inability to sing Christian music effectively by saying "they have no feel for it." The truth is that they either have not been gifted by the Spirit or else they have quenched their gift and are relying upon their natural talent.

An example would be two singers who are going to sing "The Lord's Prayer." The first, operating in the flesh, might sing the song perfectly and receive a standing ovation. The second, leaning on the Spirit, might sing the song most imperfectly and receive no ovation because the listeners are too busy weeping and repenting of their sins. The second singer has allowed himself to be an empty vessel through whom the power of God can be manifested.

It is so difficult for us to empty ourselves of self. It is particularly difficult in the areas where we are talented. We would rather trust ourselves than God.

So it was with my preaching. I wanted to wow people with my oratorical prowess. I often did. But they went away empty because I had not shown them Jesus. I had shown them me.

I struggled with this problem for several years before I experienced a breakthrough. Once again, the agent was Martin Lloyd-Jones, the man whose magazine interview had served as my third and conclusive "witness" when I was trying to decide whether I should resign my job and preach the soon return of Jesus.

Someone gave me a copy of his marvelous book on preaching. Right in the middle I found the key. He wrote, "When preparing a sermon, work on it as if everything depended upon you. Then preach it like everything depended upon the Spirit."

My sermons soon began to evidence a new power, real power, as I learned to yield to the guidance of God's Spirit in the pulpit. I lost interest in impressing people with my skills. I became obsessed with lifting up Jesus. I had learned that even when we are serving God, we need Him more than He needs us.

I quickly applied these new-found truths to the part of the sermon that I dreaded the most — the invitation. Evangelists are judged by results, as evidenced by the number of people who march down the aisle at the end of the sermon. There is, therefore, always a temptation for an evangelist to use emotional, often manipulative, techniques to get people to respond. I hated such techniques and yet, when I would finish offering an invitation, I would often feel that I had been manipulative.

I decided to turn the whole invitation process over to the Lord. I prayed for His guidance, and the answer He impressed upon my heart was to stop preaching invitations altogether. "Rely on the power of My Word and My Spirit," He told me.

I responded by changing the way I ended my sermons. Instead of shifting into an invitation plea that constituted a mini-sermon, I simply ended the sermon with a prayer. Then, following the prayer, I would announce that we were going to have a "ministry time." I would ask all those present who needed prayer for any purpose to come forward. I would assure them that no public announcement would be made regarding their need. They would be prayed for personally and privately.

The first time I tried this new approach was at a meeting in Nashville, Indiana, a picturesque village about 45 miles south of Indianapolis. It was on a Sunday morning at a very traditional church. I was extremely nervous about the new procedure. I knew it would be most unorthodox for this particular church. But I felt convicted of God to try it, and so I did.

I'll never forget the result. The Holy Spirit fell with great power, and people began to come forward by the dozens for prayer. I had never seen anything like it in one of my meetings. Frankly, I almost went into shock. So did some of the more staid members of the congregation!

The telephones must have rung off the wall that afternoon because that evening we had a larger crowd than on Sunday morning! It was obvious that many had come out of sheer curiosity. Again, the Spirit moved with great power and, again, many came forward for ministry.

The word spread that we were having a "Holy Ghost Blow-Out," and the attendance continued to grow. By the last night, Wednesday, we had almost 400 people present. The town had only 750 residents!

God has continued to bless this approach to ministry. The greatest movement of the Spirit I have witnessed to date in one of my meetings occurred at a large church in Lexington, Kentucky. It was my third meeting there, but my first since the Lord had convicted me to use the new ministry approach.

The church's leaders had insisted that I conduct an "old timey, week-long revival." I had resisted that plea. My meetings were always conducted from Sunday through Wednesday. The modern day attention span can't take more than about four days. Also, as you approach the weekend, there are just too many competing allurements for people's time.

But the church insisted, and I finally gave in, but not without emphasizing to them that there would probably be no one present on Friday and Saturday evenings.

I proved to be a poor prophet. The Spirit moved mightily each evening, anointing every aspect of the service, and the attendance grew steadily. Many responded for ministry, but not in the large numbers, proportionally, that I had experienced at the Nashville church.

Then it happened on the last night — Saturday night! To my astonishment, almost 800 people were present that evening. When the time of ministry was offered, around 200 responded! People were on their knees all over the front of the building. There was literally no place left to walk. I stopped the musicians several times and called for visiting preachers and elders to come up and help us pray with people.

When the ministry time was finally closed, the host minister made his way through the crowd at the front and stepped to the microphone. He was weeping.

"Folks," he said, "I have never seen anything like this before. I wish you could stand where I'm standing and see what I'm seeing. I see Christian Church preachers, Baptist pastors, Methodist ministers and even a Mennonite brother down here at the front praying with our people," he said.

He stopped to regain his composure. "And I see someone particularly important. I see the minister of one of the largest Nazarene Churches in our state down here on his knees praying with some of our folks."

He stopped again, called the man by name and asked him to stand.

"I want all you folks who are members of this church to take a good look at this man. He is the one who recently carried a large wooden cross down our main street, calling our city to repentance. His picture was in the paper. And everyone of you I heard talking about him did nothing but laugh and jeer. I want you to come down here tonight as soon as we dismiss and ask this man to forgive you."

It was a moving demonstration of the power of God's Spirit as people moved forward to hug a man they had ridiculed.

7) Living Out of a Suitcase

Seven years on the road will either drive you nuts or teach you how to rely on God. I spent the first three years ministering at small churches which were very concerned about expenses. That meant I always stayed at someone's house.

Usually it was some dear widow lady who was anxious to smother the visiting Evangelist with hospitality — and I mean smother! I always take a lot of work with me when I'm on the road, and I quickly discovered that it was almost impossible to get anything done at a hospitable home. The hostess was always popping her head in my room to see if I needed something.

"Do you want a Coke? How about a cup of coffee? Want some cake? How about some brownies? You've just got to try my persimmon pie!"

Bless their hearts, as they put it, "I just want to make you feel at home." They meant well, but the harder they pushed, the more uncomfortable I felt. I just wanted to be left alone.

But I would rather be smothered in hospitality than have to wallow in filth. I've stayed in some homes so filthy that I made excuses not to eat for fear that I might die of ptomaine poisoning. Honestly, at one home I stayed in, dirty dishes were stacked all over the cabinets and kitchen table. Some had been there so long they had a green fungus-looking mess growing on them. That particular house was also knee-deep in cat and dog hair, and the bathroom smelled like an open sewer. My gracious hosts seemed totally oblivious to the fact that they were living in a garbage can.

I once stayed with an elderly gentleman who I later discovered was a manic-depressive. I didn't know what was wrong with him when I was there. All I knew was that he wanted to play board games all night every night. When I would finally insist on going to bed at 12:30 or 1:00 in the morning, he would then spend the rest of the night banging around in his wood shop, practicing on the piano, or vacuuming. Needless to say, he was in his manic stage.

I experienced a contrast to his noise when I stayed with an elderly couple who absolutely refused to speak to each other. The man spent most of each day in his room with the door closed. He came out only for meals, which were eaten in deathly silence. Anything said was said through me.

"David, tell my husband to eat some more vegetables."

"David, tell my wife to mind her own business."

They had been married over 50 years, but it was a marriage in name only.

The strangest form of communication I ever encountered was at a home where the hostess talked to me through notes which she stuck on my pillow — or stuck on the wall or any other place she could find.

I arrived at her house at mid-day. She showed me the bedroom where I was to stay. I unpacked my things, took a shower, changed clothes and went down town. When I arrived back at her house, the walls of my bedroom and bath were literally plastered with those little yellow stick-on notes.

One on the shower door read, "Always close the shower door when you finish." The one stuck above the towel rack said, "Please fold your towels neatly before hanging them." There was one on my pillow that said, "You should use the other bed. This one has a hard mattress." There was even a note on the back of one of my shoes, "Please place your shoes completely under the bed." In my closet I found notes stuck to my suits telling me if they needed cleaning or pressing.

You can understand why I began to demand a motel room when I started ministering at churches large enough to afford one. Still, I found most churches wanted to avoid the expense. I would get a call from the minister — "I know you prefer to stay in a motel but ..." He would then explain that he had the ideal place in some home where he could "guarantee" that I would not be bothered.

One of those places was a "mother-in-law room" that had been built on to the main house. As the minister described it over the phone, it sounded ideal. A private entrance. A separate kitchen. A private bath. A completely self-contained unit with no door connecting it to the main house. I agreed to stay there, and sure enough, it turned out to be all that he had described. It appeared to be the perfect place for a traveling evangelist.

I settled in for the night completely content with my accommodations. About 4:30 a.m. I suddenly awoke with the feeling that someone was in the room. Someone was! It was the 12-year-old daughter of my hosts. She was just standing by the side of the bed staring at me. Since I don't sleep with much on, I was relieved to find the covers pulled up. I jerked them up even more and asked what she was doing there.

"Just looking," she said.

"But why at this time of the morning?" I asked.

"Oh, I'm supposed to be helping my brothers milk the cow."

That didn't compute. But I was soon to find out what she was talking about. The father of this family was a stickler for discipline and responsibility. He had bought his children, two boys and a girl, a cow, and it was their responsibility to get up every morning at 4:30 to milk that cow. They used the kitchen of my quarters to strain the milk. So, every morning at 4:30 the three of them would come into my kitchen with milking pails clanging. The last morning I gave up. I got up, put on my clothes, and went out to milk the cow with them.

I don't want to leave the wrong impression. Most of my hosts were delightful people who blessed me with their loving kindness. But what most people do not understand is that even in the most ideal circumstances, you can never truly relax while staying in someone's home. When you are on the road constantly, you need to stay where you can relax.

One of my preacher friends from California who has spent

many a year on the road summed it up best, "You never want to have to stay in any place where you must put on your pants to go to the bathroom!" Amen.

The funniest story I've ever heard along this line happened to a preacher friend of mine who now pastors one of the largest churches in Louisville, Kentucky. In his early years of ministry he was holding a meeting at a country church in the hills of West Virginia.

The people there had an incredible concept of hospitality. They felt that the only way to be really hospitable was to have the visiting evangelist stay at a different home each night! That meant he had to pack and unpack every day of the meeting.

Every home he stayed at that week had an outdoor toilet, which was an adventure in itself. At the last home he stayed in he decided to make the trip down the path before turning in for the night. His mountain man host went to a kitchen cabinet and pulled out a flash light and a roll of toilet paper. He handed them to my friend and pointed him toward the back door. My friend stepped outside and started walking. He said he walked a long way and still could not see the outhouse. Finally, he stopped and started shining his flash light all around him, looking for the little house. At that point, the mountain man, who was standing on the back porch, shouted, "Just out there anywhere will be OK!"

Staying in homes can be a very trying experience, but motels are not exactly the Garden of Eden. In the years since I've insisted on staying in motels, I have had some memorable experiences.

Like the time I got locked in the bathroom of my room at the Holiday Inn in Olney, Illinois. The door handle just spun around and around. Like most motel bath rooms, this one was about the size of a closet. I tend to be claustrophobic. The walls started closing in on me real fast. I tried yelling and beating on the walls. No success. I decided to wait on the maid, but then it dawned on me that it was 5 p.m. and the maid wasn't due in until the next morning. I emptied my pockets and spent the next 20 minutes using my car keys and paper clips to get the screws out of the door handle. I then jimmied the exposed mechanism to get the door open. I haven't closed a bathroom door at a motel since that time.

My wife rarely travels with me since she is a first grade teacher, but occasionally, when the meeting site is not too far away, she will go with me on Friday or Saturday and fly back home on Sunday. She went with me one weekend in late November to a meeting in the Houston area.

The man who met us at the airport told us that there was no motel in the small town where the meeting was being held. He dropped us off at a motel in a town about 10 miles away.

"This is the closest motel to our church." he explained. "It used to be a Holiday Inn, but it recently changed hands. We hope it's in good hands."

It wasn't. A classic "Texas Norther" had blown into Houston that day and it was unusually cold for that time of the year. I kept fiddling with the thermostat in our room, trying to get the heat to come on, but nothing I did seemed to work.

By bed time it was so cold in the room we simply could not tolerate it any longer. I called the front desk.

"I can't get the heat to come on in my room," I said.

"Yes, I know," said the lady. "It's off in all the rooms."

"When do you expect to get it back on?" I asked.

I will never forget her answer. There was a long pause, and then she said, "Well, let me put it this way. We are praying for warmer weather."

Translated, that meant there was no heat and there wasn't going to be any. So my wife and I put on all the casual clothes we had brought with us and got back into bed. It proved to be a long, cold night. The next morning we discovered that they also did not have any hot water. We had our bags packed and waiting when they came by to take us to the Sunday morning service.

One motel I stayed at looked like a movie set. It was a classic 1930s "tourist court." It was clean and neat, but it was old. I could have tolerated it except for one thing — there were no phones in the rooms. A phone is essential to me. I have to call my office frequently, and my wife always wants me where she can reach me by phone.

I walked up the street about a block and found a telephone booth. I looked in the phone book and noted that the town had several modern motels. I decided I would tell the preacher that I just had to have a phone and that I would personally pay the difference in the cost of the motels. I rehearsed my speech to make it as tactful as possible. I decided I would deliver it that very evening when he picked me up for supper.

Well, before I could get a word out of my mouth, he said, "We need to stop at the manager's office on the way out. The owner wasn't here when you checked in but he's there now. I want you to meet him. You see, he's one of our elders, and he always lets the visiting evangelist stay here free."

I spent a lot of hours that week in a telephone booth down the street from my room.

My greatest motel adventure took place at another classic "tourist court" in a small town nestled in the hills of eastern Kentucky. It was the only motel in the town.

As we drove to the town from the airport in Lexington, the two men who picked me up gave me a warning, "Our pastor says the motel where you're going to stay has only six good rooms. They are the ones numbered one through six. So, be sure to insist to the desk clerk that you be put in one of those rooms."

When we arrived, I followed their instructions, and I was given room six without any difficulty. The room made me wonder what the less decent ones must look like. It was outfitted in what could only be described as vintage World War II army furniture. Everything was made of gray painted steel. The carpet and drapes smelled of years of cigarette smoke. The room had only one redeeming social value. It had a telephone.

I unpacked all my clothes and called my office to tell them where I was and how to get in touch with me. That's when I discovered there was no phone number on the telephone. I looked around for a phone book but couldn't find one. I told my office manager to hold for a moment while I ran over to the office to get the phone number.

My ensuing conversation with the middle-aged lady at the desk was something out of *Alice in Wonderland*.

"What's the phone number here?" I asked.

"Why?" she responded as if I had asked some sort of dumb question.

"I need to give my office my phone number. What is it?"

"I don't know."

"What do you mean, you don't know?"

"I mean I never call it."

"Look, lady, I'm serious. I need the number."

"And I'm serious. I don't know it."

I could see I wasn't going to get anywhere with her, so I shrugged my shoulders and turned to go back to my room.

"Oh! Wait a minute!" she shouted. "Here it is on these matches."

She handed me a book of matches. Printed on the cover was the motel name and phone number.

After my phone call, I decided to take a nap. I had hardly laid down on the bed, when there was a knock at the door. It was the desk clerk lady.

"I'm sorry, sir," she said, "but you're going to have to move."

"What do you mean?"

"Well, I made a mistake," she explained. "We've got a big family reunion coming in, and they specifically reserved rooms one through six. They know these are our best rooms. So, you've got to move."

I couldn't believe that she actually admitted I was staying in one of their "best" rooms. I tried arguing with her, but her mind was set. I had to move. She handed me a key.

"It's upstairs at the other end."

Of course it was upstairs at the other end! But it didn't turn out to be as bad as I had imagined. Actually, it was just like the other room. The same interior decorator had done both. And most important, it too had a shiny new telephone.

I spent the next 15 minutes making trip after trip up and down the stairs to transfer all my stuff to the second room. Once I got everything situated, I picked up the phone to call my office again to give them my new room number. There was no dial tone. I checked the cord to see if it was plugged in. It was.

Downstairs to the office again.

"Ma'am, I'm very sorry to keep bothering you, but my phone won't work."

"What do you mean, it won't work?"

I could tell it was going to be another memorable conversation. "I mean it won't work. It's dead."

"That's impossible. We've got a brand new phone system. It was installed just last week. You just don't know how to work it."

I nearly bit my tongue off to keep from jumping on that remark. How ignorant did she think I was that I didn't know how to operate a simple telephone?

Up to the room we marched. She picked up the phone and listened. She checked the cord. She listened again. She slapped the phone on the side two or three times. She listened again.

"This phone don't work," she said confidently. "You're just going to have to do without."

"Oh no, I'm not!" I said. "I've got to have a phone, so get me another room."

Back down to the office. She gave me the key to a third room. It was upstairs next to the one I was in. I stuck the key in the lock and started to open the door. At that precise moment I heard someone yell, "What are you doing?"

I looked up. It was the maid. "I've just been assigned this room. I want to check it out."

"I wouldn't go in there, if I were you," said the maid.

"Why's that?"

"Cause there's a woman in bed in there."

I quietly pulled the key out of the lock and headed back downstairs.

"You mean that lady is still in bed? Why I thought she left an hour ago. Well, try this one," the room clerk said.

I was handed my fourth key. Upstairs again. This time I knocked first. Several times. No response. I stuck the key in and turned the handle. It wouldn't budge. I started wrestling with the knob. Along came the maid again.

"What are you doing now?" she asked.

"I'm trying to get this door open."

"Why?"

"Why? What do you mean, Why? I've been assigned this room, that's why!"

"What? I'll swear, I don't know what's wrong with that crazy room clerk."

"What do you mean?"

"Why nobody's been able to get into that room for almost three months. The lock won't work."

Downstairs again. Apologies. A fifth key. Upstairs again. I was beginning to feel like an actor in a surrealistic play.

The door opened, and there was no one in the bed or shower. So far, so good. I picked up the phone. There was a dial tone. Everything appeared in order. I started moving my stuff to the new room. By the time I finished, I had worked up quite a sweat. I decided to turn on the window air conditioning unit before I laid down for a nap.

Click. You guessed it. Nothing happened. I looked to see if it was plugged in. It wasn't. I picked up the plug, and I could hardly believe my eyes. Two of the three prongs were broken off.

I still marvel that I didn't blow my stack. It was maddening, but it was all too funny. By the time I checked into the sixth room, I was enjoying a good laugh along with the desk clerk and the maid. The sixth room proved to be a winner. But it was still World War II, and it was upstairs.

Lodging predicaments are not the only ones you face while traveling. There is also food. I once read where one of the most famous evangelists who ever lived weighed almost 400 pounds when he died. I was astonished. "How could such a godly man become such a glutton?" I thought. I soon learned when I went on the road.

There are dear sweet ladies all over this country who pride themselves in stuffing the visiting evangelist. You sit down at tables that are groaning from the weight of the food on them, and then you are strongly encouraged to have two or three helpings of everything, whether you like it or not. Just when you think you're about to pop, out come the desserts.

What's really pathetic is trying to speak after such a feast. Your spirit feels heavy and your stomach churns. Your attention focuses on trying to muffle the burps as they constantly rise to the surface. You literally don't know for sure what's going to come out of your mouth every time you open it.

I put on 20 pounds quickly and decided something had to be done. I started sending out an advance letter to the host minister explaining that I eat only two meals a day — breakfast and lunch — and that I never eat before speaking in the evening.

It didn't work. As soon as I would arrive, the minister would say, "I know you don't like to eat supper, but several of our ladies always cook for the visiting evangelist, and they insisted on preparing meals. However, they told me to tell you that you don't have to eat."

Sure. Tell me, how do you go to a sweet lady's house for supper and just sit there sipping tea when you know she's been cooking her heart out all day long? No way.

Others handle the problem in another way, "Dave, I know you don't like to eat before you preach, so we've scheduled all your evening meals for after the services."

That's even worse. When I preach, I preach with all my

physical, spiritual and emotional strength. When I'm finished, I'm really finished. All I want to do is go to bed. Instead, I often end up at someone's house eating a huge meal at 10 p.m. The result is that I end up going to bed at midnight or later — and with a full stomach which prevents me from sleeping soundly.

There seems to be no way around becoming a 400-pound evangelist. There are just too many sweet ladies who are determined to give you "just one good home-cooked meal."

Another food problem I have is that I'm a Mexican-food junkie. I love what is called "Tex-Mex." Basically, it is enchiladas and tamales smothered in chili. I rarely ever get an opportunity to eat Mexican food on the road and, when I do, it is rarely ever the "Tex-Mex" variety. When I arrive back in Dallas from a meeting, my wife always drives me directly from the airport to a Mexican restaurant because she knows I am experiencing withdrawal pains.

The third aspect of living out of a suitcase is, of course, travel. My three-year-old granddaughter has gone with me to the airport so frequently that she thinks I work in an airplane. When she sees a plane flying over, she always points and says, "Look, Mommy, there goes Paw-paw."

I'm thankful that when I first began to travel my Bible study led me to an understanding of the reality of the ministry of angels. I had heard of "guardian angels" all my life, but we had never studied angels in our church. I still remember how excited I got when I discovered Hebrews 1:14 which says that angels are ministering spirits who have been sent forth to serve those who are in the process of being saved. Wow! Angels available to serve me — what a thought.

When I saw how many airplanes were falling out of the skies, I decided to use the ministry of angels to protect my flights. I've been using that ministry ever since. Every time I get on an airplane, I pray, "Lord, please surround this plane with your holy angels and allow them to fly with us every mile of the way. May they protect us and give us a soft landing." I always conclude that prayer by asking the Lord to post an angel at my house to protect my wife.

Some of those angels have had to work overtime. I was flying one time from Dallas to Denver. When we arrived over Denver, we started circling. After circling for almost an hour, the pilot made an announcement over the intercom.

"Ladies and gentlemen, I'm sorry, but Denver is in the midst of a blizzard. We can't land at the moment, so we're going to fly to Albuquerque and sit down there for a while. Maybe the storm will blow over."

That announcement created a storm inside the plane. I soon became aware of the fact that the plane was packed with groups of skiers who were anxious to get to the ski slopes. The word "blizzard" was music to their ears. To heck with the danger. Let's land!

But, no, we were headed for New Mexico. The mood turned dark and surly. The flight attendants must have reported the situation to the captain because he soon came on the intercom with another announcement.

"Ladies and gentlemen, I know you are very disappointed, so we have decided to provide drinks on the house! Have as many drinks as you please on us, and enjoy the delay."

The liquor began to flow. The mood changed. We sat on the ground in Albuquerque for two hours, but I'm not sure anyone noticed except me. By the time we made the landing in Denver, I was the only sober guy on board. People were feeling no pain. Since I was sitting mid-way back, about half the people got off the plane before me. They were singing and laughing and carousing. By the time I got to the gate, my host minister was in a state of shock. He was wondering what I was doing on a plane loaded with drunks.

My wildest airplane adventure occurred on a flight from Dallas to Cleveland. I had held a meeting in Cleveland once before. Shortly after that meeting, I received an invitation to hold a prophecy conference in Lancaster, Ohio. As soon as I accepted that invitation, I started receiving letters from people at the church in Cleveland telling me they planned to attend. Based on those letters, I assumed that Lancaster was a suburb of Cleveland. I never bothered to check a map.

I made my plane reservations and informed the Lancaster church of my flight number and arrival time. Now Lancaster is located just outside Columbus, Ohio, about 150 miles south of Cleveland. I had a flight booked for Cleveland. The people in Lancaster naturally thought I was flying into Columbus. You can imagine how surprised the elder was who came to meet me when he discovered there was no such flight number coming into Columbus.

Since he assumed that I was smart enough to reserve a flight to the correct city, he therefore drew the conclusion that the airline had put me on the wrong flight. When he explained the situation to them, they, too, drew the same conclusion. No one suspected that I would be so dumb as to fly to the wrong city.

The airline officials began scrambling around trying to come up with a solution to "their" mistake. At one point they asked the elder if I was in any way related to President Reagan! He told them I was not, as far as he knew. They told him that if I were related to the president, they were going to radio the plane to make a special landing in Columbus! Who says connections don't count?

Meanwhile, I was flying to Cleveland, completely oblivious to my dumb mistake. When I arrived, there was no one to meet me at the gate, but that didn't bother me because most of the time I'm met at the baggage claim area. I proceeded to the baggage area and, just as I was picking up my suitcases, I heard my name being paged over the public address system.

I picked up a courtesy phone and identified myself. The lady told me to stay right there. In just a few minutes, two porters came running up, grabbed my luggage and told me to follow them. They took off at a fast clip. I had no idea what was going on.

The next thing I knew, I had been hustled into another airplane. The plane was already loaded with people when I arrived. Everyone stared at me with the obvious question written all over their faces, "Who is this guy who's been holding up our flight?" I was directed to one of only two vacant seats. My luggage was stuffed in a closet up front. I kept asking what was going on. All I was told was, "You're in the wrong city."

As we took off, I turned to the person next to me and asked where we were heading.

"Orlando," he responded grumpily.

"Orlando! You mean Orlando, Florida?"

"Yes," he replied. "This is a travel club. We chartered this plane to fly us non-stop to Disney World. Who are you and why are you on here?'

I didn't know what to say. I couldn't get past the thought of Orlando. Why had I been put on this flight? As I was struggling for an answer to his question, a stewardess came up and began to apologize.

"We are so sorry that we put you on the wrong flight."

"What do you mean?"

"You were supposed to be on the flight to Columbus. We put you on the flight to Cleveland by mistake. This is a charter flight to Orlando, but we're going to make a special stop in Columbus to let you off. Please forgive us for any inconvenience we may have caused you."

"Do you know where Lancaster, Ohio is located?" I asked.

"Oh yes," she said, "right outside of Columbus."

Suddenly it all clicked. I had booked the wrong city! They thought it was their mistake. It never occurred to anyone that I could be so dumb as to fly to the wrong city. I was so embarrassed that I kept my mouth shut and let them continue to believe it was their mistake. The result was a free ride to Columbus on a special chartered jet. "He shall give His angels charge over you, to keep you in all your ways" (Psalm 91:11 — NKJV). Thank you, Lord.

8) Maintaining a Sense of Humor

I was holding a meeting at a small church in Pekin, Indiana. One evening before the service a lady walked up to me and asked, " Do you have a sense of humor?"

"Lady," I said, "to survive in this business, you've got to have a sense of humor."

"Oh good," she said, "because I want to share something funny with you. Last night as my six year old son and I were driving home from church, I noticed that he was very quiet. 'What are you thinking about?' I asked him. 'The preacher,' he said. 'What about him?' I asked. 'Well ... he sure can preach for a bald headed man!' "

The evangelist's life may be filled with trials and tribulation, but it is also liberally sprinkled with a lot of good laughs, if you only have the sense of humor to enjoy them.

I'm convinced that God has a great sense of humor. He would have to have, otherwise He would never put up with you and me. I'm also convinced that those who serve Him must have a sense of humor to survive. The reason is that most of the laughs they will encounter will come at their own expense. It's one of the ways God keeps us humble.

I experienced an embarrassing slip of the tongue in a sermon on cults. I was coming down hard on the evils of the cults and began to name them specifically — the Jehovah's Witnesses, the Moonies, the Christian Scientists. I then dramatically said, "But the worst cult of all, the largest and best organized and the one that is leading the most people to hell, is the Masons." There were audible gasps all over the audience. I was startled. I had never received such a response before from a Christian audience to the identification of the Mormons as a cult. I paused to reflect. That's when it dawned on me that I had said "Masons" instead of "Mormons." I didn't bother to correct it. I figured it was a Holy Ghost slip of the tongue because no Christian has any business being a Mason. I found out later that there were a lot of Masons in that particular congregation. I hoped they had a sense of humor.

My verbal problems usually come when I get carried away with enthusiasm and start waxing eloquent. One evening I was preaching on the millennium. I was developing the point that when the Lord returns to reign, He will redeem the plant and animal kingdoms.

"They will be put back the way God intended them," I pointed out. "There will be no poisonous plants, no weeds and no carnivorous or poisonous animals. The lion will lie down with the lamb and eat straw with the ox."

That's where I should have stopped. But no, I had to go on and belabor the point.

"I'm hoping and praying that when God redeems nature, He will do away with the chiggers!"

It got a big laugh.

I didn't say it to get a laugh. I was serious. I hate chiggers.

For those of you who don't know what I'm talking about, let me explain. A chigger is a microscopic little critter that infests the grass during the summer months in the Southern United States. They jump on your legs, crawl up to a tender spot and then bite with such ferocity that a large, red whelp rises up that itches like mad for three of four days. They are definitely a part of the Curse.

My wife happened to be present the evening I expressed the wish that God would do away with the chiggers. As we were driving home, she was very quiet. I could feel it coming. Finally, I asked.

"What's the matter?"

"I couldn't believe your remark this evening about the chiggers," she said with a sound of exasperation.

"Yes, I know," I responded. "I guess I got a little carried away."

"Oh, that's not the point."

"Then what is the point?"

"The point is that what you said shows that you don't understand Bible prophecy."

Those were fighting words. I started to launch into a testy defense, when she cut me short.

"You see, honey," she said calmly, "God is not going to do away with the chiggers. He's going to make you lie down with them!"

We both had a good laugh, but all the time I was thinking, "If He does, I hope He defangs those little boogers first!"

The Apostle Paul once had a fellow fall out of the balcony while he was preaching (Acts 20). I've never had that happen, but I've learned to hang loose and expect almost anything to happen while I'm preaching. I've had to contend with electrical black outs, leaky roofs, crackling public address systems, screaming babies, snoring elders and even heart attacks.

Noninsulated public adress systems are one of the worst hazards. You can be right in the middle of making a crucial spiritual point when the system will suddenly pick up a CB transmission from some trucker, and the whole sanctuary will be filled with expletives of the worst sort. It's always difficult to recover from such a blow.

The funniest interruption I ever experienced occurred at a church in Jennings, Louisiana. It was on a Sunday evening. About 300 people were present. I was in the middle of a sermon on the signs of the times, when I began to notice a strange noise. It sounded at first like a low-level police siren. It was a steady, high pitched, oscillating tone. I stopped and tapped the microphone. The sound continued.

I then noticed that people near the front were beginning to get tickled. Some lowered their eyes and giggled. Others covered their faces and muffled their laughs. One man got so tickled that he started shaking all over and finally laid down in the pew.

That was it. I couldn't take it any longer. I stopped and asked, "What's the matter?"

A fellow on the back row stood up and shouted, "It's Grand-dad's new watch. The alarm has gone off, and he can't hear it!"

The whole congregation exploded with laughter as the man ran to the front, tapped the patriarch of the church on the shoulder and pointed at his new wrist watch.

It took a good five minutes to get everyone settled down again and back into the lesson. Then, believe it or not, the alarm went off again. And again, the elderly gentleman did not hear it.

The next evening when he arrived, he showed me a naked wrist and said, "Mother made me leave it at home." His wife smiled triumphantly.

Every church has one or more clock watchers. These are often stern and authoritarian sorts who are determined that no service will ever run more than 59 minutes, especially during the pro football season. They constantly check their watches in an exaggerated manner to impress a sense of time consciousness upon the preacher. They always give me the feeling that if I go one minute over time, the floor will open up and swallow me.

The most unusual time watcher I ever ran across was a fellow at a church in Dallas. I was conducting a week-long prophecy conference, and every evening this man, who was one of the elders, would come up to me after the service and complain because I had not preached long enough! I thanked him for the compliment, but I told him that I didn't want to wear out my welcome. I like to leave people wanting more. But my explanations were to no avail. He continued to complain every evening about me "cutting it too short."

On the last evening of the meeting he met me at the door as I arrived and asked if he could borrow my wrist watch for a moment. I thought it was an odd request but, before I could ask why, I was besieged by well-wishers who wanted to ask questions about prophecy. While talking to them, I slipped off my watch and handed it to the man. He promptly disappeared.

I forgot about the watch until it was time for me to preach. When I started to the pulpit, I felt for it and then remembered I had loaned it to the elder. That didn't bother me because that particular church had three clocks on the walls — one on each side and one at the back. In fact, I had never seen a church with so many clocks. It gave you the impression that the whole congregation was made up of clock watchers. I found out that appearances can be deceiving.

For you see, when I looked to see what time I was starting my sermon, to my surprise I discovered that all three clocks had been draped! There was no way for me to tell what time it was. I've been looking for a clock watcher like that one ever since. It was probably the nicest compliment my preaching has ever received.

The worship time has the potential to be even more unpredictable than the preaching time, simply because more people and equipment are involved. Music accompaniment tapes are always starting at the wrong time or else not starting at all, leaving the nervous singer facing an audience in awkward silence. There are the out-of-tune pianos, the squeaky electric organs, and the drummers who believe that loud is beautiful. There are the Sandi Patti copycats who try to mimic her beautiful singing and end up screeching on all the high notes.

There are the draggy song leaders who lead every hymn at funeral pace. There are the peppy ones who come across as frustrated cheer leaders. There are choir members who sit slack-jawed, napping on and off throughout the service, and there are others so full of the Spirit that they do everything except jump the pews and hang from the chandeliers.

Personally, I'll take enthusiasm over deadness any time. It's always easier to tone down a fanatic than to resurrect a corpse.

One corpse I vividly remember was the song leader at a fairly large church in Louisville, Kentucky. On the Sunday morning the meeting began, this character looked out at the congregation with sleepy eyes and a sour face. He issued a Marine-like command: "Everyone turn to song number 234," he barked. "That's song TWO, THREE, FOUR!"

I started turning fast in fear that if I didn't, I might receive a public reprimand.

"The name of this song," he snarled, "is 'Stand Up, Stand Up For Jesus.' But I don't want to inconvenience any of you, so we're going to sing it sitting down."

We proceeded to sing a stand up song sitting down. It was really an "inspirational" moment. By the time I got up to preach, the people were in a semi-comatose stage. I felt like Ezekiel standing in the valley of the dry bones speaking to the Frozen Chosen.

I went back to the motel and got on my knees before God.

"Lord," I cried out, "do something about that song leader. Some way or other get him out of the picture so that we can experience some real worship."

When I arrived back at the church that evening, one of the deacons called me aside. "We've got a problem," he said worriedly. "Our song leader got a call from his boss this afternoon and was told to go to Tennessee immediately. We don't have a song leader for this evening."

It was hard for me to keep a straight face. I wanted to shout "Hallelujah!" I had prayed that guy right out of the state! I assured the deacon that I knew a really good worship leader there in the city who would be glad to substitute. That evening we started worshiping the Lord.

The hardest act I've ever had to follow in a worship service was one that I ran into at a meeting in New Mexico. The church had invited a husband and wife team with a Western format to lead in worship. They were a very sincere pair, but they had come to entertain and not to lead in worship.

They dressed in cowboy clothes, performed funny skits, and

sang old-time, down-home Western songs for which they had written Christian lyrics. The congregation, particularly the children, loved every minute of it.

My most difficult moment came on the night when the man suddenly jumped out of sight behind the piano. When he re-emerged, he was wearing a "50 gallon" cowboy hat made of styrofoam. It was literally about three feet tall and five feet in diameter. He then pulled out a home made base fiddle composed of a broom handle attached to an upside down wash tub. He strummed on the fiddle and sang while wearing the monstrous hat. When he finished, he bowed to the wild applause, pointed at me and said, "And now ... here's Brother Reagan!" As I said, it was a tough act to follow.

The most memorable worship group I ever encountered was a family of Mennonites in central Indiana. The meeting was being held at an independent Christian Church, and I was surprised when the pastor informed me that he had invited a family of Mennonites to lead the worship each evening. He assured me that they were an outstanding group.

When it came time for the Sunday evening service to begin, the Mennonites had not yet arrived. The pastor was getting very nervous. He kept pacing around on the front porch of the church, looking hopefully up and down the street. At about five minutes after the hour, several pickup trucks arrived and the Mennonites jumped out carrying their instruments.

They were an interesting sight to behold. The men were dressed in dark colored work clothes and wore vests. The women wore long dresses with long sleeves and had little bonnets on their heads. But the person who caught my eye was the stern looking patriarch who led the clan. He had on overalls and a vest. He had a classic Mennonite beard and was wearing a wide-brimmed black hat. He looked like he was ready to preach hell fire.

I shuddered to think what kind of worship leaders these people might be. I figured we were in for a week of drab hymns sung like Gregorian chants.

The patriarch gruffly apologized for being late. He explained that their milking chores had taken longer than expected. The women quickly set up their instruments, then the men stepped forward to sing. The patriarch took off his hat, cleared his throat and, in a dead-pan fashion, said they were glad to be with us.

Then, he suddenly started patting his foot and snapping his fingers. "Ah one and ah two and ah three," he said rhythmically — and the whole group broke out in one of the liveliest renditions of "Old Buddha" that I have ever heard!

I was in stitches. They had turned out to be the opposite of what I had expected. They were anything but drab. "Old Buddha" is one of the funniest Christian songs I have ever heard, but it has a powerful message about the folly of legalism and sectarianism. It was the last song in the world I would have expected this group to sing.

They went on that night and the rest of the week to bless us greatly with anointed leadership in worship. They were people who loved the Lord, and it came through in the worship they led. I have always wondered if the stern patriarch was putting us on that night. I don't think he was. He reminded me of the Hassidic Jews of Israel. They take their religion very seriously. They are stern in countenance and drab in dress. But they know how to relax before the Lord and throw their whole being into the expression of joyous worship.

The next year when I returned to that same church, they again had a worship treat in store for me. The pastor had invited one of the most gifted Christian song writers and worship leaders in the country to come from Nashville, Tennessee, to both teach and lead worship. The day before the meeting was to begin, the fellow called and asked if he could bring his own piano player. The pastor agreed.

When the worship leader and his accompanist arrived, I experienced a real surprise. The pianist was none other than a young man by the name of Mark who had grown up in the same church that I had in Waco, Texas. He was several years younger than me, but I knew him well and recognized him instantly, even though I had not seen him in years.

The next day when I got up to preach, I told the congregation about our common roots in the same boyhood church. Then I made an observation: "Our presence here this morning is proof positive that God has a great sense of humor. You see, Mark and I grew up in a church that does not believe in prophecy or instrumental music. Yet, here am I preaching prophecy — and there Mark sits playing the piano. We have made a pact. I won't tell the folks back home what he's playing, if he won't tell them what I'm preaching!"

Some people strongly object to humor in the pulpit. They feel like it detracts from the sanctity of God's Word. I respect their view. I, too, cringe in response to preachers who think their major purpose is to make people laugh throughout their sermons. But I do not object to using some humor to establish rapport with the audience. It helps them to realize that you are human like them and that, although you take your message seriously, you don't take yourself all that seriously.

Because I have an earned doctorate, I am forever being introduced as "Dr." Reagan. I don't like that. It sounds stuffy, formal and religious. I always respond to the pastor's introduction by thanking him for being kind and gracious, but then I shift gears and threaten him if he calls me "Dr." again. I usually say something like, "Brother, if you call me 'Dr.' one more time, I'm going to start referring to you as 'His Holiness the Right Reverend.' " That really isn't much of a threat since most pastors would welcome that kind of respect!

I sometimes follow up that comment with one of my favorite stories. I tell the folks that every time I'm called "Dr." it reminds me of the fellow who was invited to speak to the national church convention. When he received the convention's pre-publicity packet, he noticed that every other speaker that year had a doctorate except him. He not only did not have a doctorate, he had no master's or bachelor's degrees. In fact, he was a high school dropout with only one qualification to speak — he was full of the Spirit of God.

When he started filling out the background publicity sheet that always comes with one of those packets, the devil got the best of him. He wrote down his name, paused for a moment, then put a comma and wrote, "M.D., D.D., L.L.D."

When he arrived at the convention, he quickly discovered that he was the talk of the town. Everywhere he went he overheard people talking about "the fellow with the three doctorates." They were all going to his session to hear him speak.

By the time he got up to speak, his conscience had gotten the best of him. "Ladies and gentlemen, " he began, "I must start with a confession. Those letters after my name—M.D., D.D., L.L.D.—do not stand for what you think. What they really stand for is Mersy Doates, Dosey Doates and Little Lamsey Divies!"

I am constantly kidded about being a Texan, particularly if I'm preaching in the rival state of Oklahoma. I bring some of this upon myself because during the football season I always exhort the congregation where I'm preaching to pray for the Dallas Cowboys to win that Sunday afternoon. That plea is often greeted with boos and hisses. But I quickly explain that it is in their own best interest to pray earnestly for a Cowboy victory because when the Cowboys lose on Sunday afternoon, I always preach hell, fire and brimstone on Sunday evening! I generate a lot of prayers for the Cowboys that way.

Actually, I rarely tell Texas stories because I got into big trouble one time when I bragged about Texas from the pulpit. I was preaching about Paul, and I casually mentioned in passing that Paul was one of the greatest Texans who ever lived.

After the service, an irate lady came up and challenged me. "How dare you say Paul was a Texan! What proof do you have of that?"

I explained that I really didn't have any proof. I just assumed he was a Texan because he was such a great man.

"Well!" she said in disgust. "I can prove beyond a shadow of a doubt that he was not a Texan. Read Philippians 4:11."

That passage says, "I have learned to be content in whatever state I'm in." The woman was right. Paul was not a Texan because no Texan could ever make such a statement.

At the next service I corrected my statement and shared the Biblical evidence for the correction. I asked the people to forgive me for misleading them. When that service ended another irate lady came up and said, "Paul may not have been a Texan but he was definitely a Southerner. Read II Corinthians 13:14."

That passage says, "The grace of the Lord Jesus Christ and the love of God and the fellowship of the Holy Spirit, be with y'all." No doubt about it. Paul was a Southerner.

A year later I was sharing all this with a congregation in Oklahoma. Another lady came up afterward and said, "I've got some really tough news for you. Paul was really a Sooner!"

Now that was too much. I couldn't bear the thought of the great Apostle having Okie roots. I demanded Biblical proof. She told me to read Hebrews 13:19. It says, "I urge you all the more to do this, that I may be restored to you the sooner." That's a tough pill for a Texan to swallow. More than ever, I now believe that Paul did not write Hebrews.

I find that people are often uptight about prophecy preachers coming to their church. They figure they will be subjected to a bombardment of doomsday preaching. I like to use humor from the prophetic Scriptures to put these people at ease.

One of my favorites is I Corinthians 15:51. I urge each congregation to frame this scripture and hang it in their nursery. It contains a prophecy that is fulfilled during each service. The verse reads: "We shall not all sleep but we shall all be changed."

My meetings usually end on Wednesday night. I often like to begin my sermon that evening by sharing a story about Wednesday services.

When I was growing up in the church, our preachers had an obsession with what we called "Wednesday Evening Prayer Meeting." The preachers were always trying to build up the Wednesday night attendance with different gimmicks, usually to no avail. They would almost always end up trying to motivate attendance by putting a guilt trip on us. This came in the form of a fiery sermon that left you with no doubt that you would spend eternity in Hell if you did not attend on Wednesday night. That was always effective. Wednesday night attendance would immediately shoot up, but it would begin to taper off after a few weeks.

With this background, you can appreciate one of the favorite stories of my heritage. It seems that a large group of our people were in line at the Pearly Gates, waiting to be interviewed by St. Peter. The line was very long that day, and our group was about half a mile back.

As we slowly approached the gate, we noticed something unusual. Every time a group would get to the gates, the leader would say something to St. Peter, St. Peter would respond, and the group would then go bananas! I mean they would put their hands up in the air and start dancing and shouting, "Hallelujah!"

We started getting nervous. These folks were acting like Pentecostals, and we sure didn't expect to spend eternity in Heaven with such unruly people. Finally, we could stand the suspense no longer. We appointed one of our staid elders to go up to the front of the line and find out what was going on.

We watched him anxiously as he said something to St. Peter and St. Peter replied. All of a sudden, the elder stuck his hands up in the air and started dancing in the Spirit! We couldn't believe our eyes. He danced all the way back to where we were standing, all the time shouting, "Praise the Lord!" at the top of his voice.

"What is it? What is it?" we called out.

"Oh! I've got incredibly good news," he shouted. "Guess what? Wednesday nights don't count!"

I use a lot of Scripture when I preach. People often discover books that they didn't even know were in the Bible. This extensive use of Scripture has prompted a lot of comments.

A lady came up to me one time and said I reminded her of a preacher she once knew who had a scripture for everything. She then gave a hilarious example of what she was talking about.

It seems this particular preacher had gone to visit one of his flock — a lady who had just come home from the hospital. He knocked on the door of her house and waited. He heard a door open inside and the pitter-patter of feet as someone ran across the room. But no one came to the door. He continued to knock. He continued to hear noises inside. But he couldn't get anyone to the door.

Finally, he gave up and started walking back to his car. Just as he got to his car, it occurred to him that there must be some scripture that would be appropriate for the occasion. He thought for a moment and then got an idea. He pulled out a calling card and wrote on the back of it, "Revelation 3:21." He went back to the house and stuck the card in the door. That verse says, "Behold, I stand at the door and knock; if anyone hears my voice and opens the door, I will come in to him and will dine with him and he with me."

Two days later the preacher received an envelope in the mail. Inside was the calling card he had left on the lady's door. On the back side, underneath his scripture reference, she had written, "Genesis 3:10." That verse says, "I heard the sound of thee in the garden, and I was afraid because I was naked; so I hid myself."

9) Teaching the Future

In addition to evangelistic meetings, I have held prophetic seminars all over the United States. These can be tailored to any time period, but they normally last for three to four hours on a Saturday afternoon. Again, I find that many people come to these seminars very uptight because they suspect that my purpose is to convert them to a particular prophetic viewpoint. That suspicion is often based on past experiences with other prophecy teachers.

I don't know what it is, but there is something about the nature of Bible prophecy that seems to bring out the dogmatism in people. Prophecy teachers as a whole tend to be some of the most dogmatic people on the face of the earth. They also tend to be both sensational and polemical in their style.

Thus, the typical prophecy teacher has an answer — the one and only right answer — to every question. He tends to be argumentative and debative, almost relishing a good verbal dual. He often will spend most of his time attacking the viewpoints he disagrees with, rather than presenting his own view in a positive manner. He usually traffics in the sensational, being more concerned about the Anti-Christ than Jesus Christ. It is not at all unusual for prophecy teachers to run newspaper ads showing drawings of strange, multi-headed creatures and featuring teaser questions like, "Does Jane Fonda's name add up to 666?" It's no wonder that people often shudder in horror when they hear a prophecy teacher is coming to their church!

I try to cut through all this reservoir of ill will by stating up front that I have no desire to convert anyone to a particular prophetic viewpoint. I have a particular viewpoint, and I believe in it very strongly, but it doesn't bother me in the least if someone doesn't agree with it.

My first and foremost purpose is to get people interested in studying God's Prophetic Word. It constitutes one-third of the Bible, and I'm convinced that it is the most ignored portion of the Bible.

My second purpose is to draw people closer to Jesus through their study of prophecy. If prophecy is taught properly, it will automatically do this, "for the testimony of Jesus is the spirit of prophecy" (Rev. 19:10). My third purpose is to convince people, regardless of their particular prophetic viewpoint, that Jesus is coming soon.

With respect to differences in viewpoints, I stress that what a person believes about Bible prophecy has no impact whatsoever on where he is going to spend eternity. Heaven is going to be occupied by premillennialists, amillennialists, postmillennialists, and some people who don't know the difference in a millennium and a centipede.

One of my favorite prophecy stories is the one about the four little boys at Sunday school who were trying to impress each other with their Bible knowledge. "I'm a premillennialist," said one of them. "That's nothing," said the second, "I'm an amillennialist." "So what?" said the third. "I'm a postmillennialist." The fourth boy didn't say anything. The others began to press him. "Come on, tell us what you are." "Well," he replied, "I guess I'm a panmillennialist." "What's that?" they asked. "A panmillennialist," he explained, "is a person who doesn't know what's going to happen in the end times. All he knows is that God is in control, and therefore everything will pan out in the end."

This is not to say that what a person believes about prophecy is irrelevant. All truth is relevant, and we should seek the truth in all matters. The point is that what we believe about prophecy is not relevant to our justification. The only thing relevant there is what we believe about Jesus. But our prophetic beliefs are very relevant to our sanctification — to how we live in the present.

I'm a classic example of what I'm talking about. For 30 years I knew almost nothing about Bible prophecy. I was saved because I had accepted Jesus as my Lord and Savior. But my spiritual development was in neutral because of erroneous concepts and pure ignorance regarding things like the Holy Spirit and Bible prophecy. Not once during that 30-year period did I ever yearn for the Lord to come. Not once did I pray "Maranatha!" (I Cor. 16:22) I was apathetic about the return of the Lord — and even fearful of it. After all, He might come on one of my bad days and catch me committing some sin.

My study of Bible prophecy had a transforming effect upon my life. It helped me to better understand the grace, mercy and love of God. It brought me to the realization that the Lord's return is my "Blessed Hope" and not my "Holy Terror." It also convinced me that Jesus is coming soon. That conviction had a purifying effect because it motivated me to holiness. For the first time in my life, I accepted Jesus as my Lord as well as my Savior.

Another important point I try to make at the beginning of each seminar is that a person does not have to be a walking genius in order to understand Bible prophecy. Many people have the mistaken idea that a person must have a Ph.D. in hermanuetics or a doctorate in imagination in order to understand Bible prophecy.

This erroneous concept is due to several factors. One is the vocabulary. Prophecy teachers often sound like they are speaking in tongues non-stop. "Premillennial, postmillennial, amillennial, chiliast, anti-chiliast, pre-tribulation rapture, post-tribulation rapture, and so forth." It's enough to scare anyone. I try to cut through all this technical verbiage by showing the meaning of these terms through simple diagrams.

I also emphasize that I believe the Bible was written by God for the common man to understand, with the help of the Holy Spirit. I've found that the key to understanding Bible prophecy is a very simple one: "If the plain sense makes sense, don't look for any other sense, lest you end up with nonsense." The problem with Bible prophecy is not that it is hard to understand. The problem is that it is hard to believe. If you will believe it, you will understand it.

I find that most Christians know almost nothing about Bible prophecy. Since they themselves realize this, they often come to my seminars with a rather defensive attitude. I try to put them at ease on this point by emphasizing the fact that I knew almost nothing about Bible prophecy until 15 years ago. After attending church for 30 years, I was so prophetically ignorant that I thought the Rapture was a sensation you feel when your girl friend kisses you. I would have identified Gog and Magog as the name of a comedy team. And I thought the Anti-Christ was a "denominational" preacher.

Maybe that's one of the reasons God called me to teach prophecy. I can really identify with those who have gone to church all their lives and still couldn't find the book of Habakkuk if their lives depended on it. I know how they feel. I know the embarrassment of looking for the book of Hezekiah, only to discover that no such book exists.

At my prophecy seminars, I always try to save at least half the time for people to ask questions. I used to approach this segment of the seminar with sweaty palms, but no longer. I now look forward to it with delight, mainly because I never cease to be amazed — and amused — at some of the questions people can come up with.

The three legitimate questions that are most frequently asked are the following (listed in the order of their frequency):

1) When will the Rapture occur?
2) Where is the United States in Bible prophecy?
3) Will we know each other in Heaven?

The most off-the-wall, bizarre questions I can remember are these:

1) Will we have the same pets in Heaven?
2) Will the Anti-Christ go through the Tribulation? (The normal question here is, "Will the church go through the Tribulation?")
3) Will the Illuminati fight at Armageddon?
4) Will I have to diet in my glorified body?
5) Will we recognize our enemies in Heaven?
6) How long will church services last in Heaven?
7) Is the 1,000 year "rain" of Jesus similar to the 40 day rain of Noah?
8) Will I have to lean how to play a harp in Heaven?
9) Is the pope amillennial?
10) Will a pregnant, unsaved woman's baby be taken from her womb at the Rapture?

Now you can understand why I used to get sweaty palms. But I've learned to roll with the punches, and I've also learned how to simply say, "I don't know."

One question that often comes up is, "What language will we speak in Heaven?" I always answer by saying that my best guess is Hebrew, and I give several scriptural references to back up the guess. A Mexican-American friend of mine recently heard me give that answer and he challenged it.

"Oh no!" he protested. "We are going to speak Spanish in Heaven."

"Where did you get that crazy idea?" I asked.

"Right out of the Bible."

"Where?"

He smiled. "Haven't you ever read where the Bible speaks of the 'Chicano Glory'?"

At a seminar in Louisville, Kentucky, a person asked if I knew the prophetic significance of the word, "Selah." This is a word that is found in the margin of some Psalms (for example, Psalm 24). I patiently explained that no one knows for sure what that word means — that the best guess is that it was some sort of musical notation. I added that I did not believe it had any prophetic significance.

I was about to go on to the next question when a fellow spoke up and said he thought he knew what the word meant. He said he thought it was a cuss word that David used whenever he broke a harp string! It's always a joy to receive help from the audience when trying to answer the really tough questions.

One of the most irritating questions I ever received came during the taping of a television series before a live audience. The format was for me to teach for 25 minutes, break for a 5-minute musical interlude, and then conclude with 25 minutes of questions from the audience.

We wanted to keep our editing costs to a minimum so we emphasized to the audience that they should keep their questions brief and relevant. We especially emphasized the relevant aspect since we wanted the questions to relate directly to the presentation.

On the night I spoke about the "Jew in Prophecy," the very first question from a lady in the audience was, "Do you speak in tongues?" The tape editor made a lot of money off us before we finished that series.

The only thing more weird than some of the questions asked at the seminars are some of the rumors that circulate among prophecy buffs. I'm absolutely convinced that most prophecy enthusiasts have very vivid imaginations. The thing that upsets me is the way otherwise normal people will jump upon prophecy rumors with enthusiasm and pass them along mindlessly to other people without ever bothering to check them out. Some of the favorites that I keep running across include:

1) There is a "computer beast" in Belgium that contains the names and addresses of every person in the world.

2) The vultures are multiplying and gathering in Israel in anticipation of Armageddon.

3) Henry Kissinger's name adds up to 666.

4) Bar codes will soon be stamped on our hands.

5) Social security checks will have to be endorsed with the number 666.

On and on it goes, ad nauseam. My favorite is one that still pops up from time to time. It is the rumor that the building blocks for the new Temple have been cut, finished and numbered — and that one building block is stored in each K Mart in the U.S.!

Let's hope and pray God has a really good sense of humor.

10) Filling the Airwaves

When the ministry began we had no intention of going on the radio. Our outreach was to be through meetings, seminars, cassette tapes and publications. But the Lord had a different idea.

The ministry was hardly six weeks old when one of my trustees called and said I should get in touch with a farmer in Hereford, Texas, right away. The trustee had met the farmer at a Dallas religious gathering, and the farmer had asked that I contact him.

I called the man immediately. He told me that he had heard a taped sermon of mine on the second coming of Jesus.

"Are you broadcasting that message on the radio?" he asked.

"No sir."

"Why not?"

"We can't afford to."

"Why not?"

"Well, sir, this ministry is only six weeks old. We don't have any money or equipment to use for radio broadcasts."

"Well, I'm interested in putting you on the radio. Can you come see me?"

He didn't have to ask twice. I was on my way to Hereford the next day. I didn't even know where Hereford was located. I soon found out. It's a small town on the High Plains of the Texas Panhandle. As I traveled there, I marveled at the way God had brought us together. I was to marvel even more over the ways of the Lord after the meeting was over.

The first thing I discovered on arrival was that this "farmer" happened to own one of the largest natural food companies in the entire country. Yet, he was a humble man of God with an office barely large enough for two people to sit in. We spent a couple of hours just talking about the Lord. Then he got down to brass tacks.

"Is radio expensive,?" he asked.

"It costs $60 a day in Dallas," I replied.

"That's peanuts!" he observed.

"Well, sir," I said, "it may be peanuts to you but we don't have that kind of money."

He thought for a moment, and then he said, "I tell you what I'm going to do. I'm going to give you a check that will enable you to get on the radio in Dallas. It will be 'seed money.' If God wants you to continue on the radio, He will supply the additional money. But don't ever expect anymore out of me. This is a one time gift to start a new outreach. I'm giving it because God has convicted me that He wants your message on the radio."

He then wrote me a check for $4,000! I was speechless. He had never asked me what church I attended or what creed I affirmed. He had simply heard a message that had touched his heart, and he wanted to share it with others.

Because of this man's faith and his love of the Lord, we launched a radio ministry in the summer of 1980, broadcasting over one station in Dallas. The program was called "Christ in Prophecy." It was aired daily, Monday through Friday, for 15 minutes.

For a year we broadcast only over the Dallas station. I focused on the teaching of Bible prophecy and emphasized my conviction that Jesus is coming soon.

Near the end of that first year, I began to feel the leading of the Lord to move in a different direction regarding program content. I began to speak out on national and international issues from a Biblical perspective, stressing from time to time that many of these issues are signs of the soon return of the Lord.

What God had led me to do was blend my Biblical knowledge with my professional training in national and international politics. The new format really clicked. People began to respond in dramatically increased numbers, and we began to consider the possibility of expanding the program to other stations.

Our mail made it clear that we were speaking to a real need — the need of Christians to relate their faith in meaningful terms to the world around them. Many letter writers confessed that they were bewildered by both national and world issues and needed some Biblical guidelines for dealing with the issues. I began to speak out on pornography, abortion, homosexuality, humanism, satanism and many other such controversial topics.

As I did so, both the interest and support level grew, and we began to expand to other stations. That meant making a lot of very difficult decisions. At what pace should we expand? Should we choose this station or that one?

I praise God for the wise trustees He has always blessed me

with. From the beginning of our radio ministry, the trustees insisted upon two things: first, that we would never operate in the red; and second, that we would never use air time to beg for money. They stressed to me over and over that God would supply every need of the radio ministry if we would expand it at His pace and not at ours.

That meant expanding slowly and cautiously. It meant spending a lot of time in prayer, praying about every possible addition to our growing network of stations. It meant looking earnestly for signs of God's will in every situation. Sometimes those signs were subtle. At other times they were very dramatic.

One of the most dramatic occurred when I called WXLN in Louisville, Kentucky. I asked to speak to the station manager, but he was not in. I was directed instead to a salesman. I introduced myself and told him I was interested in putting our program on his station. He started giving me his sales pitch. Suddenly, he stopped in mid-sentence and said, "What did you say your name is?" I repeated my name. He asked if we had ever met. I told him I didn't think so. "Well," he said, "your name sure is familiar." He went on with his sales pitch.

Then, again, very suddenly, he stopped his presentation and started shouting, "Hallelujah! Hallelujah!" I thought the poor fellow had lost it.

"What's the matter?" I asked.

"Oh praise God!" he shouted. "I can't believe this."

"Believe what?"

"I knew your name sounded familiar," he said. "I just glanced at my prayer list and your name is on it."

"How could that be?" I asked.

"Weren't you on The 700 Club about two months ago?"

"Yes, I was."

"I thought so!" he replied. "I was sick that day and stayed home. I saw you interviewed, and God impressed upon my heart that I was to pray for you and your ministry. I've been doing that every day for almost two months. And today you call me!"

By that time I was shouting, "Hallelujah!" To me, it was certain confirmation that we were to put our program on his station.

Not long after that I received a call from the manager of station KAJN in Crowley, Louisiana. He had heard our program over a Houston station, and he wanted it on his station. I wasn't interested. I wanted to reach as many people as possible and that meant spending our money on stations in large urban areas. Crowley is a little country town. I wasn't interested in broadcasting to chickens and cows.

But the Crowley manager was very persistent. He kept calling and calling. He just wouldn't take no for an answer. I asked the Lord for clear direction, and it came loud and clear.

First, I received a mailing honoring J. Vernon McGee's fortieth anniversary in Christian broadcasting. Here was one of the most honored men in Christian radio, broadcasting daily over more than 300 stations. A testimony from Dr. McGee was enclosed and a sentence in that testimony caught my eye. He said that of all the stations he was broadcasting over, that three were particularly effective — and one of those was KAJN in southern Louisiana!

Two days later I received the second sign. A lady living in Crowley called me and said that if I would put our program on KAJN, she and her husband would donate $250 a month. The program has been on KAJN since that time.

Not all the decisions have been that easy. There have been times when we have missed the Lord's leading. But overall, the Lord has blessed our program, and we have been able to keep it on the air for over seven years.

Hardly a week goes by now that we do not get at least three calls from stations wanting our program. The offers are always very enticing. The first month free. The second month at half price. The third month at two-thirds price. Four months before we have to pay the full rate. It is so easy to say yes and start running ahead of the Lord. It's really no wonder that so many radio and television ministries are so deeply mired in debt.

I remember a visit I had several years ago from a good friend who had just started a radio ministry. He asked how many stations I was broadcasting over.

"Oh, I think about 12 or 15," I said.

"What's the matter with your program?" he asked.

"What do you mean?"

"Haven't you been on the air for five years?"

"Yes."

"Well, I've been on for only six months and I'm already broadcasting on over 30 stations."

Of course he was. I could have been on 100 stations. But a day of reckoning comes when the bills start pouring in. Within a month that particular minister was not on any stations. He had run ahead of the Lord.

The first five years of our radio ministry we ended every month with all our bills paid. That was a real miracle, particularly when you consider how we operate. Every day we offer something free on the program like a cassette tape or a publication. We tell people to send a donation, if they can, but we stress that it is not essential. The items really are free.

We might open 25 letters in a row requesting a cassette tape and not a one of them have anything in them except an apology for not being able to send a donation. Then, the 26th envelope will contain a check for $250 from someone we never heard of. That donation will pay for their request and all the others.

We never experienced any serious financial problems in our radio ministry until January of 1986 when the bottom fell out. It was like everyone forgot we existed for one month. The result was that when we got to the end of that month we did not have enough money to pay *any* of our radio bills.

I went into a period of soul searching. Was I personally out of God's will? Had the ministry moved out of the Lord's purpose? Were we running ahead of God? I prayed and sought the Lord, and in the process I became convicted that we were being put to a test. I felt like the test was related to two things.

Beyond a doubt it was related to a courageous decision the

board had made the previous year. The board had stepped out in faith and voted unanimously that during 1987, the seventh year of the ministry, I was to take a Sabbatical rest from my travels. They asked me to stay home for one year and devote myself to study, prayer and writing. We normally receive at least $50,000 a year from love offerings at meetings and seminars. That income would have to come from other sources during the Sabbatical Year. No one knew where it would come from. They were just going to trust the Lord to supply.

I marveled at the board's faith and rejoiced over their courage. I knew God was calling the ministry to a year of preparation for greater service in His kingdom than I had ever imagined. I knew, too, that the decision would infuriate Satan.

For that reason, I could see Satan's handprint all over the financial crisis of January 1986. It was as if he were taunting us, trying to shake our faith in the Lord, with the hope that we would waver and surrender the commitment to the Sabbatical Year.

I also saw that crisis as a second kind of test. I felt that the Lord was using it to see if we would be faithful to our dual commitment to never operate in the red and never use radio time to beg for money.

The board stood firm in all of its commitments. The trustees never waivered on their decision to use 1987 as a year of rest, even when the financial crisis worsened in the summer of 1986. And they never hedged on their other principles. We cut our number of stations more than in half to adjust to financial realities. There was no begging on the air. There were no desperate appeals. The stations were simply cut.

Cutting the stations was not easy to do. In fact, it hurt. It was like losing dear friends you had visited with every day for years. Listeners were shocked and outraged. We were deluged with mail asking where we had gone. We sent out explanations of our policies. We were deluged with mail again, filled with apologies for taking us for granted and not supplying us with the gifts needed to keep us on the air.

It was a tough year, but God gave us the victory. We ended the year on a handful of stations but with all our bills paid for the seventh calendar year in a row. By the end of that year we were beginning to add back some of the stations we had cut.

The radio ministry has been a constant source of joy and encouragement to me. When I'm feeling the least bit down, all I have to do is pick up a batch of radio mail and start reading the marvelous letters that come in from listeners all over the country.

In response to a broadcast on racism, a black woman from Denver wrote: "Hallelujah! Thank you brother Reagan ... I would like to inform you that I have adopted you as my 'Dad.' Would you be so kind as to send me a picture of you for my family photo album?"

A 14-year-old girl in Sulphur, Louisiana, wrote a heart-touching request: "I listen to you on the radio every chance I get and it is a big blessing. Please pray for my father, mother and brother. They do not go to church and they do not see the way of the Lord and how close it is to His coming."

A lady in Richmond, Kentucky, wrote words of encouragement: "I enjoy your program very much. I used to listen to Paul Harvey at 12:30 p.m. each day, but since I started listening to your program, I have not had the desire to listen to Paul again even though he has a very good program."

Especially thrilling are the testimonies about spiritual experiences. A lady in Stanford, Kentucky, wrote these words in response to a tape that was sent to her: "You are in part responsible for my accepting Christ, as I did so after listening to your tape, 'Jesus is Coming Soon.' "

From Lafayette, Louisiana, came these moving words: "On my day off this week I turned on the radio and heard you discussing the Second Coming. I immediately felt the anointing of the Holy Spirit and fell to my knees in prayer and thankfulness to Jesus my Lord and Savior. Tears rolled down my cheeks and, for the first time, I could actually see the astounding light and absolute glory of Jesus descending from Heaven and being crowned King of the Universe. Brother Reagan, at that moment I received a joy in my spirit and in my whole body and mind that nothing and no one will ever be able to dim or take from me."

In response to a broadcast on homosexuality, I received an encouraging letter from a man who had been delivered from this bondage: "I listen to your program each time it is broadcast and I truly enjoy it ... I especially enjoyed your talks on homosexuality. I am a former homosexual whom God has redeemed, and it is good to know that someone is on my side ... I praise God that He has removed me from such a hideous problem and has put me back on a road of righteousness."

I have devoted many broadcasts to the problem of abortion, which I consider to be the number one problem in America. In response to those broadcasts, I have received many powerful letters from women who have had abortions, and I have read many of these over the air, without identifying the authors. The result of reading one such letter was to bring healing and reconciliation to a family in Sunset, Louisiana:

"Greetings in the name of our Lord and Savior Jesus Christ. I'm writing to tell you about the blessing the Lord brought about in my life through your radio program.

"I wrote to you before about the mistake I made in having an abortion. On June 19 you read my letter on your program. You may recall that I wrote that my parents did not know about my abortion. I have wanted to tell them about it for a long time, but I just couldn't bring myself to do it.

"Since my mother and father listen to your program every day, I knew that more than likely they would hear my letter on your show. [We always notify people in advance as to what date we are going to use one of their letters on our program.] So I prayed to the Lord that either they would not hear your program that day or else they would hear it and it would help them understand. I just told God to have His will.

"Well, my mother did hear the letter and knew it was from me. My parents were so understanding and forgiving. I feel so free now that it's out in the open. I know the Lord has forgiven me and I feel He will use me in helping other women and maybe somehow I can save the lives of some of the unborn babies that are being slaughtered every day."

That's what I call a "block-buster!"

We receive a lot of humorous letters. One of my favorites came from a man in the hills of West Virginia who wrote: "I have a lot of trouble getting your telecast on my radio."

Another favorite came from a lady in Wichita, Kansas, who said she listened to the broadcast every day with her four year old daughter: "I knew my daughter was a great fan of yours," she wrote, "but I never realized how much until last night. At the end of her bed time prayer, she said, 'And thank you God for Jesus, brought to us by Lamb and Lion Ministries.' "

One letter that really amused me was motivated by my constant appeals for Christians to do something about the problems of our society. I point out that we are to be the salt of the earth and that means we are to stand up and be counted for righteousness.

I urge people to pray for God to lay a burden on their hearts for some social problem and then to pray for God to tell them what to do about the problem.

A lady in a large metropolitan area wrote and said she had prayed and prayed for God to show her something to do. She said He had finally given her a great idea. She explained that her job was to daily test about 20 cars for one of the country's leading car rental companies. "As I drive each car along the test route," she wrote, "I set the buttons on the radio to each Christian station in our city. Everyone who rents one of our vehicles gets a car with a radio tuned only to Christian stations."

Sometimes people are a little ambivalent about the program. A lady in Beaumont, Texas, wrote: "I love your show. Actually, I thoroughly disliked it at first because I figured sooner or later you'd start on the 'end-time-Armageddon-scare-you-out-of-your-wits' stuff or else start getting really militant about denominational doctrine."

Another fellow from Owenton, Kentucky, expressed the same sort of ambivalence in more direct terms:

Lamb and Lion
Thrills me
Chills me
But most of all
Fills me
With the Spirit of Jesus.

People are always writing to find out which church the ministry is affiliated with. They can't seem to believe that there really is such a thing as a non-denominational ministry. One lady wrote a compliment in this regard that really blessed me: "I'm very happy to be able to say that after several months of listening, I still don't know what kind of church you belong to. Thank you for that! It proves to me that your interest in the Word of God is simply that, an interest in the relevancy of the Word to today and the future."

In the Dallas area, radio listeners are always calling to ask what church I pastor. When they are told that I do not pastor a church, they often ask if I will recommend a church to them. That is always difficult to do. I usually respond by asking what sort of church they are looking for.

One lady who called looking for a church said she wanted a "Charismatic" one and that it had to be located in Richardson, Texas. I told her I did not know one first hand in that city that I could recommend. She insisted that I recommend one anyway. I suggested she go to an Assembly of God. She said she wanted a non-denominational church. She continued to insist that I give her a recommendation. I finally remembered that I had attended a minister's luncheon recently where I had met the pastor of a new, independent, Charismatic church in Richardson. I gave her the name of the church.

That recommendation was to get me in big trouble. I learned never to recommend a church I have not personally attended.

About two weeks later I returned to my office from a meeting tour. My office manager told me I had received a call from an irate woman who wanted me to call her right away. She was upset about a church I had recommended. I recognized her name and remembered which church I had sent her to. Before calling her, I called a minister friend who I knew was familiar with the church.

"Tell me about that new church in Richardson," I said.

"Oh, you mean the barf-bag church?" he replied.

"Barf-bag church! What do you mean by that?"

"They specialize in exorcising demons," he explained. "When you walk in they hand you a towel and a bag, and then during the service they try to get you to vomit up your demons."

I accused him of putting me on, but he insisted that the church really did practice the vomiting of demons. I nervously called the lady. The moment I identified myself, the woman started raving. "You're not going to believe what happened to me. When I walked in the door they handed me a towel and a bag ..." The detailed description of the antics that followed still makes me nauseous.

I often put aside commentary on current events and spend a week or two just answering questions about Bible prophecy. The letters I get in response to the prophetic broadcasts are always stimulating, to say the least. People are often prompted to share experiences they have had with some prophecy fanatic. A lady in Lawrenceburg, Kentucky, wrote about such an experience in response to a broadcast I made about the Jews in prophecy: "I must admit that for many years I was ignorant of the Jew's continuing role in earthly history. Churches don't seem to talk about this very much ... I've only heard one preacher give comprehensive lessons on Revelation; and he was so caught up in it all, the only thing he talked about was 'beast this,' and 'beast that.' I began to have nightmares about weird-looking beasts of every color, size and form! I wasn't afraid of the end times because I knew I was saved; but this brother had beasts on the brain, and he put them in my brain too."

As the radio ministry began to expand, I soon became burdened down by the flood of mail. I wanted to read each letter and respond personally to the many who wrote asking for prayer and counsel. But there are only so many minutes in each day. I asked the Lord for help, and He soon provided it. I was able to hire a sensitive man of God to oversee the mail ministry. I continued to survey all the letters we received, but this man took over the responsibility of responding to those requesting prayer or counseling. It quickly proved to be one of the most effective aspects of our ministry, as attested by the following letter from a listener in Longmont, Colorado: "Dear Mike: I received your letter today telling me that you would be praying for me to find God's direction in my life.

"I wanted to write and let you know that in all my years I have been writing and sending money to various ministries, this is the first time I have ever received a handwritten, direct reply to one of my letters. Praise God for your ministry. It really does my heart good to know that God still has servants out there who take a personal interest in people. I'm not putting other ministries down because I know that they are doing great things for the Lord. But this letter from you is like a breath of fresh air to my spirit."

Not all the mail we receive is complimentary. We get our share of hate mail and crank letters — even poison pen letters that are unsigned but claim to be written in "the love of Jesus." I've been called every imaginable name, as well as a few that are unimaginable and unprintable. One letter was addressed to "That Big Shot, Know-it-all, So-called Preacher."

One thing that always produces an avalanche of hate mail is any negative comment about the King James Version of the Bible. I have discovered that there are legions who are ready to fight to the death in defense of the Bible that was "good enough for Paul." Some people even strenuously object if you read from any version other than the King James.

Another topic that always produces a lot of critical mail is any reference to ill health. All I have to do to guarantee a bunch of

negative letters is to mention that I'm suffering from hay fever
or a cold. The friends of Job are quick to respond: "Of course
you're suffering from hay fever. That's because you confessed
that you have it. If you would confess that you don't have it,
then it would go away."

A variation on the theme states: "I can't believe that a Man of
God would admit over the radio that he is ill. Don't you know
that all illness is due to sin? If you will confess your secret sins,
God will heal you." It's enough to make you really sick.

One particularly memorable negative letter was prompted by a
misunderstanding of something I said. Each time we add a new
station to our network, I always explain that we are a faith ministry. In part of that explanation I usually say, "I'm personally on
a fixed salary that is determined and supplied by my board. That
means that everything you contribute to the ministry is used for
outreach."

Some man thought I said "fat" salary instead of "fixed" salary. He wrote, "Praise God, I've finally found an honest radio
evangelist who is willing to admit that he is on a fat salary!" I
got him straightened out real fast.

Another misunderstanding of something I said led to a flood
of mail. I advertised a free tape called "Sects and Denominations." For days were were literally knee deep in letters requesting a copy of the tape about "Sex in the Denominations." I'm afraid our tape was a great disappointment.

A lot of these misunderstandings are due to the fact that I talk
fast. I naturally speak at a rapid pace and talk even faster on the
radio due to the time constraints. One person compared my radio
delivery to the "speed of a machine gun shooting full blast." I always end each program by giving the name of the ministry and
our mailing address. Because I'm talking so rapidly, many people have a difficult time understanding the name of the ministry.

The result is that we get letters addressed in very strange
ways. Here are some of my favorites:

Lanolin Ministries

Land of Lions Ministries
Land of Limes Ministries
Lam 'N Lynn Ministries
Lame Loan Ministries

The most frequent mistake is "Lemon and Lime Ministries." I guess people think we are in the fruit juice business. My all time favorite was the letter addressed to "Lame and Blind Ministries." I thought the fellow must be hard of hearing. He wasn't. He didn't like our program, and he had misstated our name on purpose as a clever sort of editorial comment.

For several years the ministry was located in a Dallas suburb called Plano. Everyone in Texas has heard of Plano because the town grew from 2,000 to 100,000 in 25 years and, during that growth spurt, the high school won the state championship in football in every division. But no one outside of Texas seems to have heard of Plano.

When we would give our mailing address on the radio, people would evidently do a double take on the name of the town because we got mail addressed to all sorts of strange places — like "Plane'O, Plain'O and Plain Old."

My favorite garbling of the name came from a lady in Illinois. We got the letter because the zip code was correct. Otherwise, we would never have seen it because she addressed it to "Playtex, Texas!" I guess she thought we were in the girdle business.

One thing that's fun about a radio ministry is traveling around the country and meeting listeners face to face. The Lord uses these encounters to keep me humble. The conversation usually goes like this:

"You mean you're the fellow on the radio?" the listener asks in obvious unbelief.

"Yes, I am. What's wrong?"

"Your voice sounds so much younger than you look!"

A variation on the theme is for the person to exclaim: "But your voice sounds like you have a lot more hair!"

The funniest comment I ever received about my voice came in a letter from a student at Texas A&M. He wrote: "I'm not sure how old you are but you sound at least middle-aged. It does my heart so much good knowing there are older men and women out there who are still hot for God. I hope and pray I get hotter as I get older."

The most memorable and touching experience to come out of the radio ministry occurred during a meeting I was holding at a large church in Lexington, Kentucky. A few months prior to the meeting, I had done a special week of radio broadcasts on the topic, "What Happens When You Die?" We had offered the material contained in those broadcasts on both a cassette tape and in printed form.

The broadcasts evidently spoke to a real need because we received thousands of requests for the cassette and the brochure. Unknown to us, one of the persons who had written for copies of the brochure was the chaplain of the Lexington Police Department.

On the second or third night of the Lexington meeting, as the pastor of the church was about to dismiss the service, the police chaplain stepped forward, identified himself, and asked permission to say a few words to the church. He explained that he had been ministering to a police officer who was dying of cancer. He had tried to bring the officer to Christ, but with no success. One day as he started driving back to the office from the hospital he heard one of my broadcasts on the topic, "What Happens When You Die?" He stopped and called our office and asked my staff to send him some copies of the brochure immediately.

When he received the brochures, he took one to the dying officer. A few days later the officer told the chaplain he wanted to accept Jesus as his Savior. He did so and died shortly thereafter.

After telling this story, the police chaplain called me up and presented me with a framed watercolor drawing done by one of Lexington's policemen. It shows a person lying wounded in a street with a policeman kneeling beside him, ministering to him.

In the background, looking over the policeman's shoulder is Jesus. The picture is entitled, "His Brother's Keeper: Christ Marks the Fall of a Sparrow." There is an inscription on the picture that reads: "Dr. Reagan: Thank you for your letter and prayer for the salvation of our sergeant."

That picture hangs in my office. It is an everyday reminder to me of the effectiveness of radio in reaching people for Jesus.

11) Adventuring Abroad

In the summer of 1984 I was given an opportunity to go to Eastern Europe and spend several weeks preaching and teaching. As is always the case with such spiritual adventures, I ended up learning a lot more than I was able to teach.

As I prepared to depart, I started requesting that individuals and churches pray for me. The response was almost unanimous: "No, we're not going to pray for you. We are going to pray for your translators!" No one believed that any translator could keep up with my rapid-fire style of delivery. They were right.

I learned quickly that working through a translator can be a most frustrating experience. I had to change my whole style of speaking. I had to speak slowly, distinctly and in simple, short sentences. I also had to avoid idiomatic expressions. It was not at all unusual to be interrupted in the middle of a sentence by the translator who would stop me and ask what a particular word meant. While we were discussing the word with each other, the audience was waiting for the translation. By the time we would get settled on a translation of the word, I would have lost my train of thought. It was maddening.

I remember preaching a sermon from Habakkuk. It was entitled, "Tough Faith." I had been speaking for about 20 minutes and had used the phrase, "tough faith," at least 50 times, when the translator suddenly stopped me and asked, "What does the word, 'tough,' mean?" I couldn't believe it. What had he been translating for 20 minutes? I never found out.

Of course, the whole translation process was further complicated by my Texas accent and colloquialisms. Some Eastern Europeans who prided themselves in their good English wondered aloud if I was really from an English speaking country! "What do you mean," they would ask, "when you say you are 'fixin' to go to town? What does 'fixin' mean?" Needless to say, we had a lot of good laughs over me trying to explain "y'all," "surenuff," "yonder" and other weird Texan slang expressions.

But the Eastern Europeans were polite and patient. They were willing to sit through any inconvenience to hear a message from the Word of God, even one they might not fully agree with. For example, when I preached a rather long sermon on the Holy Spirit, the translator turned to me at the end, smiled, bowed and said, "That was very nice but we do not agree with you." He repeated his statement to the audience, but then he asked them to thank me for coming. They gave me a standing ovation. I thought to myself, "What a contrast to the States. There I would have been lynched for preaching a 'doctrinally unsound' sermon."

My visit to Eastern Europe certainly impressed upon me the fact that we Americans take so many of our freedoms for granted. I was there under the auspices of a very experienced American missionary group, and we had to follow strict rules that they had developed through years of experience with Communist repression.

One cardinal rule was never to notify any congregation in advance that we were coming. I thought this rule was rather strange at first, but I soon found out that it is essential. It is necessitated by the fact that almost every worship service is monitored by some member of the secret police. If a minister says something the policeman considers "out of line," then the minister is called to the Communist Party headquarters the next day and interrogated.

Likewise, if a Westerner appears as a guest speaker, the minister and all officers of the church are likely to be hauled in for interrogation. If it is discovered that they officially invited the Westerner, their congregation may suffer reprisals. But if they can truthfully say that they did not know the Westerner was coming and that they invited him to speak only out of courtesy to a visitor, they will usually be left alone.

So, my guide and I would always arrive unannounced a few minutes before the service was scheduled to start. The moment I was introduced as an evangelist, I would be invited to speak, no questions asked. Their eagerness to have me speak always impressed me.

We went to all kinds of churches. Half of the time I didn't even know what kind of church I was in. But they were equally ignorant about me. All they knew about me was that I was an evangelist. That was enough for them. "Just preach the Word," they would say.

Again, I was impressed with the contrast between their attitude and that which exists here in the States. We are too concerned about doctrinal differences to invite any stranger to preach or teach. The person must first be put through a denominational inquisition to determine that he bleeds Presbyterian or Baptist or Methodist before he will be allowed to open his mouth in behalf of Christ.

The Christians in Eastern Europe understand who the enemy is. We don't. We have carefully constructed denominational walls to prevent ourselves from becoming contaminated by those who do not agree with us on every nuance of doctrine. We abuse our freedom by lobbing doctrinal hand grenades over the walls at each other.

Another rule we had to follow at all times was to be very careful about what we said out loud during unguarded moments. We were told to assume that all hotel rooms were bugged — and I'm talking about electronic devices and not bed bugs! We were therefore never to talk to one another in a hotel room about our contacts in Eastern Europe.

We never drove to a contact's residence. All cars in Europe

have a decal on the back that identifies their country of origin. Our car had a decal from a Western country. If we parked that car in front of a contact's residence, a neighbor would immediately call the secret police because the police give rewards for such surveillance. So, we would try to park in a public area about half a mile from the contact's home and then walk. As we walked, we were told to hold conversation to a minimum because, again, if someone heard us speaking in English, they might follow us to our contact's residence and then report our visit to the police.

The Communist countries like to brag about their freedom of religion. But it exists on paper only. Ministers and churches are under constant watch. Churches cannot broadcast services. Times and places of services cannot be advertised in newspapers or anywhere else. The agents are always at each service taking notes. If a minister says anything the agent considers critical of the state, the minister may find himself either out of a job or reassigned to a small country church in the middle of nowhere.

Because the worship services are monitored, very few men attend church. They fear they will lose their jobs or else lose any opportunity for promotion. Thus, most Eastern European churches are composed of elderly people, women and children. Most of the churches practice head covering for women and, since the churches are primarily composed of women, the typical view from one of their traditionally elevated pulpits is a sea of white — made up of white scarfs on the heads.

One thing the churches in Eastern Europe do not worry about is church attendance. The churches are packed to the rafters for every service. The people are hungry for the Word, and they never forget that the next service may be the last one the State will tolerate.

Again, I was impressed with the contrast to our country. Here, because we take our freedoms for granted, the church has grown fat and lazy, and ministers spend most of their waking hours trying to dream up gimmicks to promote church attendance.

One of the highlights of my visit to Eastern Europe was the two weeks I spent on the outskirts of Vienna at a large chalet nestled in the foothills of the Alps. It was a storybook setting. The chalet had been converted into a training center for Eastern European preachers.

I spent two weeks at this place teaching Bible prophecy to a group of about 15 senior pastors from Rumania. Rumania is the most repressive of all the Eastern European countries. For example, it is a capital offense to own an unregistered typewriter in Rumania.

The government tightly controls all religious activity. There is only one Protestant seminary in the country. This seminary receives on the average about 100 applications per year. The government will allow the seminary to accept only 10 students. Since no person is allowed to pastor a church unless he is a seminary graduate, the government greatly curtails church growth by only allowing 10 ordinations per year. Most of the ministers I worked with were trying to pastor five to seven churches each, using a bicycle to travel between each one!

The insidious attitude of the Rumanian government toward Christianity was illustrated in two events that took place about the time I was tutoring the Rumanian ministers.

The government discovered that one of the largest Baptist churches in the country had exceeded its building permit for a new addition by one meter. So, the government ordered the entire church to be bulldozed to the ground!

At the same time the government was trying to get most-favored-nation trade treatment from the U.S. To stifle congressional criticism of its religious repression, the Rumanian government announced that it was going to allow the importation of several thousand Bibles. Later, it was revealed that the Bibles had been sent to a paper mill and had been reprocessed into toilet paper!

The institute officials where I taught were actually shocked that the Rumanian government had agreed to allow 15 ministers to come for training. They were even more shocked when the

ministers arrived with their wives! This was totally unprecedent-
ed. Although the institute always invited the wives, the Rumanian government would never allow them to come. The wives were, in effect, held as hostages to make certain that their husbands
would return home.

The Rumanians themselves were astounded over their government's action. They had been informed only the day before
their departure that they would be allowed to bring their wives
along. Since they could not imagine the government allowing 15
couples to leave the country unattended, they naturally suspected
that someone within their group was an informer and, for that
reason, it took almost a week before we were able to get the
ministers to open up and say very much.

I'll never forget when we took all of them to the one and only
Western style shopping mall in Vienna. Each couple was given
$100 to spend. They simply did not know what to do. There
were too many goods and too many types of each item. They
were not accustomed to making shopping decisions.

As one man put it, "When we go to buy shoes at home,
there's only one style, only one color and, often, only one size."

Several of the ladies simply broke down and wept over the
cornucopia of Western goods displayed before their eyes.

One particularly distraught woman turned to me and said,
"It's all a waste because the border guards will steal whatever
we buy." Oh how we take America for granted!

The Rumanians loved to sing, and each meal with them in the
institute's dining hall began with beautiful songs of praise to the
Lord. I've never seen people savor coffee like they did. They
would linger after each meal and sip the coffee with great relish
until the dining hall lights were turned out. I discovered the reason for this is that coffee sells for $60 a pound in Rumania!

After two weeks of teaching them several hours a day, I got
to know some of the ministers pretty well. Near the end of the
second week we were sitting around one evening chatting with
each other through a translator. One of the senior ministers said
he wanted to ask a question but was afraid to do so because I

might think he did not appreciate our hospitality. I urged him to go ahead and ask his question.

To say the least, his question caught me off guard.

"When," he asked, "are you folks going to serve us some wine or beer?"

I told him he would have to ask the institute's directors, but I said that I did not think they were going to be offered any wine or beer.

"Why not?" he asked incredulously.

I tried to explain that many Christians in America did not think it was a good Christian witness to drink alcoholic beverages. They looked at each other and shook their heads as if to say, "What ignorant people!"

The next night we were once again sitting around chatting and drinking coffee after a meal. Someone mentioned something about smoking, and I expressed my appreciation for the fact that none of them smoked.

They looked stunned. I asked what was the matter. They explained that smoking is a horrible sin and that no one can be saved who smokes.

"Now that's very interesting," I observed. "Most of you call yourselves Baptists. Back in the States, many of our Baptists smoke, but they believe you will go to hell if you drink wine or beer. You believe just the opposite. Isn't that funny?"

There was a long moment of silence. Then, one of the ministers said, "No, it's not funny. Your Baptists are wrong!"

When I left for Eastern Europe that summer I was in the midst of a spiritual struggle over sin in my life. The Holy Spirit was doing a mighty convicting work within me, and I was resisting His work.

The battle inside me continued all the time I was in Eastern Europe. I felt like Paul in Romans 7 where he wrote about his spiritual struggle. He said he knew what was the right thing to do, and he willed to do it, but he ended up doing the very thing he hated. I knew how Paul felt and, like him, I kept crying out, "What a wretched man I am!" (Rom. 7:24).

After I finished my preaching tour in Eastern Europe, I returned to the institute's chalet on the outskirts of Vienna to rest for a few days before flying home. One morning I decided to take a rather strenuous hike. I climbed a steep, 2,000-foot hill behind the chalet and started walking through a thick forest. The forest was so dense that there was very little underbrush — just a thick covering of leaves on the ground. In fact, the forest was so dense that it filtered out almost all light, and I had the eerie feeling of walking in the night during daylight.

As this darkness enfolded me, so did a spiritual darkness. I suddenly became aware of an evil presence. Never before had I encountered such a satanic reality. I had difficulty breathing. I stopped walking and began taking deep breaths. I noticed an incredible stillness. There was no wind. No movement of leaves. Just deathly silence. A whisper would have sounded like a thunder clap.

Then I experienced the most intense spiritual struggle of my life. A voice began speaking to my spirit, "You're worthless. You're a sinner. You're hopeless. You will never change. You're an embarrassment to God. You've got to get out of the ministry."

Charge after charge was flung at me, all loaded with judgment and condemnation. I was overwhelmed by the vehement accusations. I fell to my knees and began to weep.

"It's true, Lord," I cried. "I am a sinner."

"I know," said the Lord. "Sinners are all I have to work through."

"But Lord, I am worthless."

"I know," the Lord replied, "but you're precious to me because you're one of my children."

"But you're hopeless," said the evil voice, "and you're going to bring down your ministry in shame."

"You're not hopeless," said the Lord. "Remember My love and the power of My Spirit."

With those words, a verse came to mind: "He who is within you is greater than he who is in the world." I summoned up the

Spirit within me, and by His power I began to rebuke the devil. Then I began to cry out to the Lord in the name of Jesus for deliverance.

"Oh, Lord," I cried, "I just want to serve You. If I can't do that with complete integrity, then I want You to take my life."

That's all I said, but it ended the struggle. The evil presence dissipated. My spirit was flooded with joy and peace. Scriptures began to race through my mind. "All things work together for good for those who love the Lord." "There is no condemnation for those who are in Christ Jesus." "Trust in the Lord, for He is an everlasting Rock, and He will keep you in perfect peace."

I opened my eyes. It really was nighttime. The struggle had seemed to last only minutes. But I had been there for hours. A gentle breeze was blowing, refreshing my being, even as the Lord had refreshed my spirit.

That night, as I prepared for bed, I opened the Bible and read these words: "The eyes of the Lord move to and fro throughout the earth that He may strongly support those whose heart is completely His" (II Chron. 16:9).

In the fall of 1985 the Lord opened another foreign door of opportunity for me. I was suddenly invited to go on a fact-finding mission to South Africa, together with a group of 20 other ministers. I quickly rearranged my schedule of meetings and, before I knew it, I was in Johannesburg, at the southern end of the world.

I had traveled throughout Asia, Europe and the Middle East, but this was my first real trip into Africa. I had been to Cairo, but I had considered it more Middle Eastern in nature than African.

I was fascinated by the incredible beauty of South Africa. Cape Town, in particular, stole my heart. Never have I been so awed by the majesty of God's creative ability. At Cape Town He outdid Himself!

But I was even more impressed by the people of that land. The variety is remarkable. There are Whites, Blacks, Coloreds (mixed races) and Indians. Then, there are varieties within these groups. The Indians are divided by religion. Most are Hindu, but significant numbers are Muslim and Christian. The Blacks are divided into 10 major tribes, each of which have a different language, culture and religion. Even the Whites are divided between the Afrikaans-speaking of Dutch descent and the English-speaking of British descent.

But something impressed me even more than the geography and the people. It was the openness of the people to the Gospel. Never have I encountered such a hunger for God's Word. The people of that land, people of all colors, are reaching out to God with open hearts and child-like faith, and God is responding by pouring out His Spirit. All that the newspapers report is racial violence, but the real story of South Africa is that the country is ablaze with the fire of the Holy Spirit. Spiritual renewal is sweeping the land, and with it is coming a breakdown of racial barriers.

I first experienced this spiritual awakening in the coastal city of Durban. I was invited to speak to an Indian congregation that met in a back room at a factory. About 200 people were present. They stood for an hour and sang songs of praise, scripture songs that were familiar to me. Then I preached for an hour on the soon coming of Jesus.

When I finished my sermon, I didn't know what to do. I had forgotten to ask the pastor in advance if he wanted me to issue an altar call. I paused, looked at him, and asked what I should do. "Whatever you feel led of the Lord to do," he replied.

I knew nothing of their traditions, and I didn't want to offend them in any way. I didn't know what to do, but I did feel led to offer a time of ministry. I explained to them what I meant by that term — that they were invited to come forward for prayer for any need that might exist in their lives. I had no idea how they might react.

We stood and started singing, and there was a stampede. People began to rush to the front. I was pressed up against the pulpit. I pulled myself free from their reaching hands and stepped up on the podium to get a better view of what was happening. I looked over their heads and saw no one. All 200 had come forward for prayer! For the next hour I prayed individually with these people for physical healing, jobs, the healing of marriages, and the forgiveness of sins.

When I returned to my hotel room completely exhausted, I sat there and wept over the contrast between that church and the typical American church. These people were like children, wanting all that their Heavenly Father has to offer.

Most Americans are so full of spiritual arrogance that they would not go forward for prayer if their lives depended on it — and that is often the case! I've seen people in American crusades who were under so much conviction that they would weep and shake all over, but they would hold on to the pew and refuse to budge, as if their feet were in concrete.

I returned to the States with a heart for South Africa. I wanted to return with a crusade team to preach the soon coming of Jesus to churches all across that country. I shared the vision with my staff, and they agreed that it was from the Lord. We began raising money to pay for the trip. God wondrously provided, and in August of 1986 ten of us departed Dallas for South Africa.

But Satan had other ideas. He was not the least bit excited about our trip. We were supposed to arrive in New York City at 6:15 p.m. and catch an 8 p.m. plane to South Africa. We touched down exactly at 6:15 p.m., but as we began to taxi toward the terminal, the pilot came on the intercom system and said, "Welcome to Harrisburg, Pennsylvania." My heart sank. There were only two flights a week to South Africa, and we were about to miss ours.

We sat on the ground in Harrisburg for two hours waiting for clearance to proceed to New York. A severe thunderstorm had knocked out the control tower computers, and all in-bound New York traffic had been either grounded or re-routed. We finally arrived in New York at 9:30 p.m. Our plane to South Africa had already departed. We were taken to a run-down hotel where we spent two hours in the lobby with several hundred other stranded people trying to get rooms.

By midnight, when my wife and I finally reached our room, I was mentally, physically and emotionally drained. I didn't know what to do. I checked with the airlines and found there was only one other direct flight to South Africa that week. It was in three days and was overbooked. We were stranded. I cratered.

But, praise God, we had with us in our group some ladies who were real prayer warriors. They never took their eyes off the Lord. While I sat in my room and felt sorry for myself, they gathered in another room and began to pray. They came out of that prayer meeting filled with conviction that it was the Lord's will for us to go to South Africa and, if we would trust in Him, He would find us a way to get there.

One of the ladies took me aside and said the Lord had given her a scriptural insight during the prayer meeting. She opened her Bible to Luke 8:22-26 and pointed out the story of the disciples who had been caught in a storm on the Sea of Galilee. As they fought to keep their boat afloat, Jesus slept. Finally, they awoke the Lord and told Him they were about to perish. He rebuked the wind, and the storm calmed. He then turned to the disciples and said, "Where is your faith?"

I thanked her for the insight. It seemed to fit our situation perfectly, and it reassured me that the Lord would see us through if we would only lean on Him. Before she walked away, I said kiddingly, "Yes, the Lord got them across the lake, but don't forget what happened when they reached the other side."

"What's that?" she asked.

"They encountered a man who was filled with demons."

"Oh dear!" she said. "Let's hope that doesn't happen to us."

The next morning the airlines called and said they had arranged for us to fly to Johannesburg via London! The Lord had prevailed. It took us an extra day to get to Johannesburg and, when we arrived, we were dog-tired, but we got there and the Lord mightily blessed our proclamation of His Word.

We preached from one end of the country to the other in all kinds of churches. It was a richly rewarding experience.

One of my sweetest memories is a service we conducted at a

small church in the heart of Zululand. The service was held at the town hall and was attended by people of all races.

The town hall and all the rest of the buildings in the town were owned by the only business in the area, a sugar cane refining factory. It was a classic "company town." All the Zulus lived in company houses and worked in the refinery. Because a visiting evangelist was speaking that morning, the British manager of the refinery had come to the service even though he was not a professing Christian.

Most of the Zulus sat at the back because an interpreter translated my message for them. When I offered the time of ministry, the first person in line was an ancient Zulu warrior who wanted prayer for chest pains. When I finished praying for him, I looked up and, to my astonishment, the next person in line was the British aristocrat who owned the town.

"I've got a bad heart," he said.

I prayed for God to heal his heart, both physically and spiritually. I'll never forget that picture of the British gentleman standing patiently in line behind the old Zulu warrior, waiting his turn for prayer. What a leveler the Gospel is!

We began and ended our crusade tour in Johannesburg. When we returned to that city for the last three days of ministry, I discovered that the scripture the lady had shared with me in New York had been prophetic. Yes, we encountered a demon-possessed man.

We were invited to minister in a remarkable setting. We had run across an American mission that had bought an apartment house with 75 units. In each apartment was a person this mission had picked off the streets of Johannesburg. There were prostitutes, drug addicts, insane, mentally retarded and physically handicapped. Never had I tried to minister to such a menagerie of people.

I had with me a remarkable worship and praise group called River of Life, and I turned over the bulk of the last two services to them because I had observed at the first service that these people were really ministered to by music. The approach worked and we experienced a powerful movement of God's Spirit.

On the last day, the missionary who directed this unusual ministry called me and asked if I had much experience in exorcising demons. I told him no and asked why. He explained that he had a young man living at the complex who was demon possessed and that he was having great difficulty trying to cast out the evil spirit. He asked if I would help that evening following the service. I told him about all I could do was pray. He said that would be helpful.

I had never participated in an exorcism, so I approached this experience with some degree of apprehension. I believed in the reality of demons and demon possession. I had done a lot of reading on the subject. I had even discussed it in some detail with an Indian minister in Durban. He had pointed out to me that exorcism had to be a major part of any Christian ministry in Africa because demon possession is so common there. The Indian people open themselves to demonic spirits through Hinduism and its pantheistic emphasis. The Blacks are subject to demonic invasion because so many of them are involved in ancestor worship and the worship of snakes.

The subject for our exorcism turned out to be a young British man in his mid-twenties. The pastor told me that they had found him wandering the streets in a totally disheveled condition. He had acted insane, and they assumed he was suffering from some sort of mental breakdown until they took him to a worship service. He had reacted immediately and violently to the mention of the name Jesus. The pastor knew then that he was dealing with a spiritual problem and not a mental one.

The pastor explained that he and his associates had held several exorcism sessions with the man and, although the man had shown much improvement as a result of their love and prayers, they had not been successful in exorcising the evil spirit.

The session began with the young man sitting on a couch. Four of us sat opposite him in chairs formed in a semi-circle. He appeared calm and rational. The pastor asked him if he wanted the demon out. He said yes. The pastor assured him that the demon would come out sooner or later.

The pastor turned to me and said, "We don't know why this demon hasn't come out but we do know one thing. The Lord is using this to draw all of us closer to Him. Forty of us are currently praying and fasting in this man's behalf."

The pastor then turned to the man and asked if he was ready to begin. He said he was. The pastor leaned forward and said in a voice of authority, "Demon, I command you in the name of Jesus to manifest yourself."

Immediately, the man began to convulse. His eyes rolled back and then closed. His body shook. His face began to distort grotesquely. His lips formed into a sneer, and then a horribly vile voice, gutteral in nature, began to come forth. The voice uttered all sorts of obscenities and profanities.

"Stop it!" the pastor snapped. "In the name of Jesus, I command you to stop this nonsense and tell me your name."

For the next 30 minutes the pastor labored to get the demon's name. The demon would evade the question by changing the subject, or shouting blasphemies, or telling lies. From time to time we would just stop and pray for guidance and faith and courage.

At long last the demon told us his name. It was Ashron. When we asked what the name meant, the demon said, "Power."

The pastor turned to me and said, "That's why we've been having so much trouble. This is a particularly strong demon, probably the type Jesus said could only be cast out through much prayer and fasting."

The pastor then called the demon by name and commanded him to come out of the man in the name of Jesus. The demon began to give excuses. He said he couldn't find his way out, that the man didn't want him out, that the Lord really wanted him to stay inside. Evasions, lies and excuses continued.

The pastor changed the subject. He asked the demon to tell him what sin he was rooted in.

"Masturbation," was the reply. The pastor shook the young man, told him to open his eyes, and asked him if he was in bondage to the sin of masturbation. He said he had been for years but that one of the staff members had prayed with him about it the previous week, and God had instantly released him from the bondage. The pastor said he wanted all of us to pray about the matter again. We did, and then the pastor commanded the demon to manifest himself.

Again, the pastor asked what sin the demon was rooted in. When he answered "Masturbation," the pastor called him a liar and commanded him to tell the truth. He then began giving frivolous answers like card playing and stealing cars.

By that time the session had lasted three hours. We were all exhausted and were getting nowhere. The pastor decided to call it quits for the night.

But before he did, he turned to me and said, "I want you to see something we've discovered."

He explained that in their exorcism sessions they had discovered that the supernatural world takes the symbolic language of the Bible very literally.

"Watch this," the pastor said. He picked up a Bible and held it in front of the young man. (Keep in mind that this man was sitting there with his eyes tightly closed and his face distorted). "In the name of Jesus, I come at you with the 'sword of the Spirit,' " the pastor shouted. He thrust the Bible at the man. The man went wild. He started backing up on the couch, flailing his arms about and shouting hysterically, "No! No!"

After he had calmed down, the pastor picked up another book. Once again he shouted that he was coming at the demon with the "sword of the Spirit." He thrust the book, but nothing happened. The man just sat there calmly.

"What book is that?" I asked.

"I don't know," said the pastor. He looked at the title. "It's a volume of the *Millennial Harbinger* by Alexander Campbell. I guess the demons don't respect Campbell."

The next day this pastor told me something very sad. He said that although exorcism was one of their main ministries, they could not reveal that to any of their supporting congregations back in the States.

"They just wouldn't understand," he said, shaking his head sadly. "They would think we had lost our minds."

He's right. Most American Christians have rejected the supernatural so completely that they no more believe in the reality of demons than they believe in the Man in the Moon.

One final note about South Africa. Every congregation we ministered to over there was integrated. The love of Jesus working in people's lives is breaking down the racial barriers within the Body of Christ.

I was so impressed with this that I made note of it in the last sermon I delivered in the country to a large congregation in Pretoria.

Here's what I said:

"I think it's ironic that we in the States spend so much time condemning you people as 'racists.' Every church I've ministered to in this country has been integrated. Yet, I often minister to churches in the States for six months in a row and never see anything except a sea of white faces."

May God have mercy upon us for our hypocrisy.

12) Walking in the Footsteps of Jesus

I made my first pilgrimage to Israel in 1979. It was a life-changing experience. It brought the Bible alive for me. It drew me closer to the Lord. Before I went, a minister friend who had already taken the trip told me that it would be worth three years of seminary. He was right.

As I stood on the Mount of Olives that first time and looked down over the majestic city of Jerusalem, I felt in my spirit that I truly was standing at the "center of the earth" (Ezek. 5:5 and 38:12).

Here the Lord God Almighty had come in the flesh to pour out His blood on a Cross for the sins of man. And right here He had ascended into Heaven with the promise that one day He would return to the same spot to rule from Mount Zion over all the nations of the world.

On that first trip I was drawn like a magnet to the Mount of Olives. Every time there was a lull in the group's schedule, I would hop a taxi and go to the Mount to meditate, pray, study scripture, or just sit and soak up the sights and sounds of the City of David.

On the last day of the tour, I got up at three in the morning and took a taxi to the Mount again. I wanted to see the sunrise, to see the city come to life before my eyes.

It was a cold morning. I sat in the Jewish cemetery on the side of the Mount and shivered as I waited for the first glimmer of sunlight to break over the Mount behind me and strike the golden dome on the Temple Mount.

I heard roosters crow.

Donkeys brayed.

Bells rang at a distance. Slowly the city was awakening. Then the first ray of brilliant sunshine hit the Temple Mount. It was morning. In my soul I had become a Jerusale-mite.

I have returned to Jerusalem many times since then, and the thrill of experiencing that wondrous city has never faded. It is new each time. There are always new discoveries to be made, new insights to be gleaned. I actually get homesick if I don't get over there at least once a year.

Part of the ministry I founded a year later has been to share the experience of the Holy Land and Jerusalem with other people who are seeking a deeper walk with the Lord. I have taken two to three groups a year to the land of the Bible. Each time, my spirit has been enriched.

We usually fly directly to Tel Aviv, spend the first night there and then head north up the coast toward the beautiful port city of Haifa. Our first stop is always the ancient Roman port of Caesarea, where the Apostle Paul was imprisoned for two years. Only a small portion of Caesarea has been excavated. One of the discoveries is a magnificent amphitheater that sits right on the coast, facing the Mediterranean Sea.

I always take my groups to this site to conduct a devotional and sing some songs. One year, after we had finished the devotional, I turned the group loose to wander for 30 minutes among the excavated ruins. I decided to just sit and look out at the ocean and meditate. While I was doing so, I picked up my Bible and opened it. The passage it fell open to was Isaiah 11.

Verse 10 caught my eye. Isaiah is speaking about the end times and he says that in those days "the root of Jesse" will stand as a "flag for the peoples" and the Jewish remnant will return to the land from "the four corners of the earth."

I looked up. Directly in front of me, about 100 yards away, there was a flagpole sticking in the sand near the water line. On it was the flag of Israel. I studied that flag for a moment, and then I began to rejoice. I suddenly realized that on that flag was the symbol of "the house of Jesse" — the star of David. That flag was serving as a magnet to draw the Jewish remnant from the ends of the earth, just as Isaiah had predicted. That is the excitement of modern-day Israel. It is a place where ancient prophecies are being fulfilled in our day and time.

One of the most breathtaking places of grandeur in all of Israel is the Sea of Galilee. It is one of the few places central to the life of Jesus that has not been spoiled by man. There are no gaudy cathedrals or sleezy shops, and the lake itself has been protected from pollution. It is easy to imagine it looking in the time of Jesus exactly as it looks today. And it is easy to understand why Jesus loved it so much that He centered His ministry in the seaside town of Capernaum.

One of the highlights of any visit to Israel is a cruise across the Sea of Galilee. I always have the boat stop in the middle of the lake and, to the rhythmic sound of the waves lapping against the sides, we sing hymns and conduct a devotional. The devotional, of course, always focuses upon the story of Jesus and Peter walking on the water.

I like to end that devotional by reading a powerful poem written by Carl Sandburg entitled "Epistle:"

> *Jesus loved the sunsets on Galilee*
>
> *Jesus loved the fishing boats forming silhouettes against the sunsets on Galilee*
>
> *Jesus loved the fishermen on the fishing boats forming silhouettes against the sunsets on Galilee*
>
> *When Jesus said: 'Goodby, goodby, I will come again ....'*
>
> *Jesus meant that goodby for the sunsets, the fishing boats, the fishermen, the silhouettes all and any against the sunsets of Galilee.*
>
> *The goodby and the promise meant all or nothing at all.*

At the point where the Jordan River exits from the Sea of Galilee there is a beautiful baptismal site that was built by the Israeli government in the early 80s. That has always amused me a little — the thought of a Jewish government building a special place for Christian baptisms. I had the special privilege of baptizing my dad at this site shortly after it was constructed.

When I first started taking groups to Israel, no such baptismal facility existed. For centuries, pilgrims had been baptized in the Jordan as an expression of their faith, and most of those baptisms had taken place at the traditional site of the baptism of Jesus, a place near Jericho at the southern end of the Jordan River. But since the Six Day War in 1967, that place has no longer been accessible to Christian pilgrims because it is located in the "no-man's land" between Israel and Jordan. So the Christian baptismal site shifted north to the only place on the Jordan that was safe from sniper fire.

The first time I went to Israel I was privileged to go with an experienced leader. He had a special place on the Jordan near the current permanent site where he always conducted his baptisms. When our bus arrived at that site, there were about 30 Jews using it for a picnic. Our leader, who had a heart for Jewish evangelism, jumped at the opportunity to witness to these people.

The leader and all those to be baptized went upstream about 50 yards to a thickly wooded area where they could not be seen by the picnickers. They stripped to their bathing suits, waded out into shoulder deep water and started walking downstream toward the picnic area — a line of about 20 Gentiles. As they approached the picnic site, the Jews stopped all their activities and stared at the line of human ducks, wondering what was going on. Meanwhile, I had slipped up behind the unsuspecting crowd and, on a prearranged signal, when our leader raised his hand in the air, I started reading in a loud voice from Matthew 3 — the account of the baptism of Jesus.

The moment I finished reading, our leader baptized the first person in the name of *Y'shua Hamashiach* — Jesus the Messiah. He proceeded to baptize every person in the name of the Messiah of Israel. Everyone then waded up to the shore, introduced themselves to the Israelis, and gave each of them a pamphlet showing how Jesus fulfilled the prophecies of the Hebrew scriptures. Amazingly, none of the Israelis got angry. I think they were too stunned by it all to know how to react!

Heading south from Galilee to Jerusalem, I always like to stop in the Valley of Jezreel, better known as the Valley of Armageddon (Rev. 16:16). We usually climb to the top of a steep tell which covers the ancient city of Megiddo so that we can get a panoramic view of the whole valley. This view is always awesome to me. It is the largest valley in all of Israel, and it appears so serene, for it is lush with agricultural production year round. Yet, it will be the site of man's last battle, the site where the blood will run as deep as a horse's bridle for a distance of 200 miles (Rev. 14:15). As we stand looking out over this apocalyp-

tic valley, I always like to read the Old Testament account of the
war that will be fought there:

> *Multitudes, multitudes in the valley of decision!*
> *For the day of the Lord is near in the valley of de-*
> *cision.*
> *The sun and moon grow dark,*
> *And the stars lose their brightness.*
> *And the Lord roars from Zion*
> *And utters His voice from Jerusalem,*
> *And the heavens and the earth tremble.*
>
> Joel 3:14-16

The climax of any pilgrimage to Israel is, of course, the city
of Jerusalem and, for that reason, I always leave it for last.
There are so many special places in that city, but there are three
that I particularly love.

The first is the Eastern Gate. I can always hardly wait to see
it. It is special to me for several reasons. For one thing, it is
what got me interested in the study of Bible prophecy.

During the Six Day War in 1967 I read a newspaper account
about the Jewish commando group that broke into the city. Ac-
cording to this account, the group first contemplated the idea of
blowing open the Eastern Gate. They knew that such an action
would catch the Jordanians by surprise. But the leader of the
group was an Orthodox Jew who strenuously objected to dyna-
miting the gate.

He was quoted as saying, "That gate must remain closed until
the Messiah returns."

He won the argument, and they proceeded to the Lion's Gate
where the Jordanians were waiting for them. The Jews suffered
heavy casualties, but they were finally able to break through the
gate and take the old walled city of Jerusalem.

I was intrigued by that newspaper article. I wondered where
in the world that Jewish soldier had gotten the idea that the Eastern Gate has to remain closed until the Messiah comes. I turned
to my Bible and, with the use of a concordance, I finally traced

down his Biblical source to Ezekiel 43 and 44 where it is clearly prophesied that someday the Eastern Gate will be closed and that it will remained closed until the Messiah comes.

That passage drove me to the history books. I discovered that the Eastern Gate had been bricked up by command of Suliman the Magnificent when he rebuilt the walls of Jerusalem in the mid-1500s. Legends abound as to why he did that, but no one knows for certain the reason. All we know for sure is that it fulfilled the prophecy of Ezekiel, and the gate has remained closed since that time — for over 400 years.

By the time I made all these discoveries, the Holy Spirit had me hooked on Bible prophecy, and I have been a student of it ever since. So you can understand my special feeling for the Eastern Gate. To me, it is proof positive that the Bible is the revealed Word of God and that God is faithful to keep all His promises. The gate excites me because I know that just as God closed it, someday He will open it when He sends His Son again.

Another very special place to me in Jerusalem is one across the Temple Mount from the Eastern Gate. It is what Christians refer to as the Wailing Wall. The Jews call it the Western Wall. (They use the term "wailing wall" to refer to the building that houses their internal revenue service!)

This site is the most sacred place on the earth to Jews. It is part of the massive wall that supports the Temple Mount. It is sacred because over the centuries it has been the only part of the Temple area that the occupying forces would allow the Jews to approach. The eastern wall of the Temple Mount cannot be accessed by the Jews because it has a Muslim cemetery all along in front of it.

The northern wall and most of the western wall have buildings built right up to them. The same has been true of the southern wall throughout most of history. Only one small section of the western wall, a section about 50 yards long has been historically accessible to the Jews and, until recently, houses were built up to within a few feet of it, creating a narrow, alley-like corridor where Jews could approach the wall and pray.

Today this area has been cleared of obstructions, and Jews come from all over the world to pray and celebrate special events like bar mitzvahs. Every time I approach that wall with a prayer cap on my head, I feel like I am intruding upon sacred ground that has been set aside for God's Chosen People. I approach it with reverence and with tears. I weep for the veil that is over the eyes of the Jewish people (II Cor. 3:14). I pray for the salvation of the Jewish remnant (Rom. 11:25-32). I also pray for the peace of Jerusalem as we are commanded to do in Psalm 122, knowing full well that when I do so I am really praying for the return of Jesus because the Word reveals that Jerusalem will never enjoy peace until the Prince of Peace returns (Isa. 62:1-5 and Zech 2:10-13).

The third place I cherish in Jerusalem is the Garden Tomb. It is a site outside the old city, about two blocks north of the Damascus Gate. It was discovered in the late 1800s by a British army general who was a prophetic scholar and an amateur archeologist. He felt that the traditional Catholic site of the Crucifixion, the Church of the Sepulcher, could not be authentic because it did not fulfill Biblical typology which pointed to the crucifixion occurring on some part of Mount Moriah, the place where Abraham offered Isaac. That Mount is in part occupied today by the Temple area, but an extension of it runs to the north and constitutes an area outside the old city that is historically known as Jeremiah's grotto.

It was in this area that the British general observed an unusual imprint in the side of a hill that appeared to be a giant skull. Knowing that the Bible referred to the crucifixion site as "Golgotha" (the place of the skull) and recognizing that this site was part of Mount Moriah, the general asserted a claim for it as the true place of the crucifixion of Jesus.

Scoffers challenged him to show them the tomb which the Bible says was located "near by" (John 19:41-42). Excavations were conducted and, sure enough, a first-century tomb of a rich man was found nearby.

The excavations also revealed that the area around the tomb had been a beautiful garden. An evangelical British group purchased the site and restored the natural beauty of the garden. They also specified in the deed that no church or monument could ever be built on the site. The site is therefore unique, for it is one of the only places in Israel that is associated with the life of Christ where some monstrous church has not been built. It is a place of quiet beauty where you can go in the midst of a busy city and meditate and pray without distraction.

The only sound you will hear besides the chirping of the birds in the trees will be an occasional hymn sung by some group conducting a communion service. It is a place of peace in the Lord.

Taking a pilgrimage group to Israel is an experience that will either develop within you the virtue of patience or else drive you to drink. You feel like a mother hen, constantly counting heads and forever worrying about the health of each person.

Israel has the finest guides in the world. They are highly trained, they are very professional, and they have twice the patience of Job. They have to have a lot of patience because Americans are some of the world's worst tourists. We want everything to happen on time with the least possible inconvenience. The result is that we are always complaining about something — usually something inconsequential. Another problem is that the average American has little historical or geographical knowledge. The result is a constant barrage of inane questions.

On one trip I conducted, a lady asked our guide, "Why are there so many Jewish-looking people in this country?"

I turned red for her and looked for a seat to climb under. But the guide never got the least bit ruffled.

He just answered politely, "It's because this is the land of the Jews."

"Oh, I see," said the lady, "that makes sense."

In another group I had a lady complain to the guide about the fact that we had been in Israel for almost two weeks and had not yet met the Ayatollah Khomeini! I was mortified. The guide never blinked an eye. "I'm sorry, ma'am," he said, "but the Ayatollah lives about 2,000 miles from here."

The Holy Land contains many layers of civilization — Canaanite, Greek, Persian, Roman, Byzantine, Crusader, Arab, etc. For the average American, this is all just too much to absorb. After about two days of historical lectures, people's eyes start glazing over when the guide mentions any aspect of history outside the New Testament context. One guide I often use refers to this glassy-eyed state as "the Historicals."

Perhaps the greatest test of patience comes from the short American attention span.

I'll never forget an incident in this regard that occurred on my first visit to Israel. We were en route to Masada and, when we reached the Dead Sea, the guide had the bus driver stop on the side of the road. The guide then proceeded to deliver a detailed lecture on the Dead Sea — its length, width, depth and mineral content. When he finished, he called for questions. So help me, the very first question was, "What is the name of this body of water here beside the bus?"

Every group has its collective personality, but every group seems to have at least one of several special types of individuals. One is what I call "the independent cuss." He's the one who simply cannot conform to any schedule. He's always late to meals and always late to the bus. He never stays with the group when visiting a site. He wanders off when the guide is lecturing and then expects the guide to later repeat the lecture just for him.

The most independent fellow I ever had travel with me was a medical doctor from Kentucky. He nearly drove me crazy trying to keep up with him. He could disappear faster than any person I've ever known — and he never left a trace as to his whereabouts. We left many a site without him, never knowing whether we would ever see him again. I rejoiced all the way home when that tour was over, mainly because he actually showed up for the return flight home.

You can imagine how appalled I was when he signed up for the very next trip. I just didn't know what I was going to do with him. On that trip we went first to Egypt and, sure enough, he disappeared on the first day in the heart of Cairo, one of the world's most congested cities. We looked for him for over an hour and finally found him standing outside the Cairo Museum engaged in a spirited debate with an Egyptian cab driver over who was the greatest — Sadat or Lincoln.

At that point I decided to turn him over to the Lord. I gave him his ticket home and told him he was free to do what he pleased as long as he showed up for the flight home. I hardly saw him again. I didn't worry about him anymore, and he had a ball. He even managed to spend a night in a Bedouin tent with some Bedouins he met on the side of the road. I figure he must have had a special flock of guardian angels.

Another type you find in every group is the complainer. I'm not talking about someone who complains occasionally. I'm talking about professional murmurers who are direct descendants of the ones who drove Moses up the wall. These are people who complain from sunrise to sunset about everything — the hotel room, the food, the weather, the water, the seat on the bus. You name it and they don't like it. These people can turn a whole group sour if you don't deal with them quickly and firmly.

All one of these complainers needs is a legitimate complaint, and they will freak out. This happened once in a group I was taking from Egypt to Israel. Admittedly, Egypt is not a tourist paradise. It is a paradise for a complainer, and we had one in the group. By the time we reached the Egyptian border, this lady had everyone's nerves on edge, complaining about a million and one trifling things that did not amount to a hill of beans. Then it happened. She was handed a legitimate complaint on a golden platter.

We had finished checking through Egyptian customs. We

lined up to march across the border single file to the waiting Israeli bus.

Just as we started moving, a very excited Egyptian grabbed
me by the arm and started shouting, "Wait! Wait!"

That seemed to be the limit of his English vocabulary so I
went back to an official I knew could speak English. He conferred with the man and then said that each of us would have to
pay an exit tax of $5 each.

I protested and pointed out that our Egyptian travel agent
(who had disappeared) had already paid the exit tax.

The two conferred again. "This is a special exit tax," the man
announced.

It was special all right. It was nothing but a shakedown.

Our professional complainer started crowing. "This is outra-
geous!" she shouted. "Never in my life . . ."

I pulled her aside and told her to keep quiet. I got our group
in a huddle and explained the situation. I told them there was
nothing we could do about it, so we might as well pay and be
done with it. I told them I knew the price of the tour was supposed to cover all costs, including taxes and tips, but this was
an unexpected cost, and I did not have enough extra money with
me to cover it. So, I asked each of them to pay their own $5 fee.
Our complainer went into orbit. She had just never heard of anything so unreasonable. We all ignored her and paid our fee. It finally dawned on her that if she wanted out she would have to
pay up, so she did.

When we arrived at the bus on the Israeli side, she was livid.
You would have thought I had personally planned the shakedown. For miles she continued to complain at the top of her
voice, heaping abuse on me and the Egyptians. Finally, one of
the men in the group could take it no longer. He turned around
in his seat and yelled back.

"Lady," he said, "you should be shouting Hallelujah rather
than complaining."

"What do you mean?" she asked in surprise.

"Because we got the best of those Egyptians," he explained.

"How do you figure that?" she asked.

"Because they left a lot of money on the table. You see, lady, I would have been gladly willing to pay $150 to get out of that lousy country!"

That shut her up — for a while. But when the trip was over, I received a letter still complaining about the $5.

"It's the principle of the thing," she wrote. I sent her a check for $5. She returned it. She just wanted to complain.

A third category of pilgrim that is present in every group, usually in abundance, is the shopper. These are the people who could care less about where Abraham slept or where Jesus preached or where Joseph is buried. They just want a bargain. They start hyperventilating when they see a street vendor or spot an Arab shop. When they discover that any shop in Israel will accept either a credit card or a personal check, they think they've died and gone to Heaven.

The Arab shopkeepers are some of the world's best bargainers. They are never in a hurry. They like to begin with treats like coffee or fruit juices to make you beholden to them. Then they move in with the flattery, kissing the ladies on the cheeks and complimenting them on their beauty. All the time they are talking about their "Christian faith," explaining that they always give a special 50-percent discount to "brothers and sisters in the Lord." The 50-percent discount is, of course, off a 300- to 500-percent markup.

But most people go away thinking they've gotten a great bargain. Both sides end up happy, and I guess that's what is important.

One of the funniest bargaining scenes I ever witnessed took place in a shop on the outskirts of Bethlehem. A lady in my group was bargaining very hard for a ring, and she was using every ploy — feigning disinterest, walking away, waving money in her hand. My curiosity finally got the best of me. I walked over and asked how she was doing.

"Great!", she said. "I've really 'jewed' this guy down on his price."

It was out of her mouth before she realized it. She whirled around to the sales clerk and said, "Please excuse me for using that term."

"That's all right, lady," he said smiling. "I'm an Arab!"

On another occasion, when a clerk quoted this same lady a price, she asked, "Is that in your money or real money?" Sales clerks in Israel also have to have a lot of patience.

One of the neatest groups I ever took to Israel was one composed of 20 ministers. It was the first trip for each of them, and they were brimming over with excitement. The group loved to sing. I think they literally sang all the way over and back and, while we were in Israel, they sang almost non-stop every moment the guide was not talking.

The longest bus trip we take in Israel is the day we drive from Tiberias on the Sea of Galilee to Jerusalem. If we go down the Jordan Valley, as we often do, there is not much to see nor are there many historical sites to visit. Consequently the guide usually has little to say. For most groups, this is a day to catch up on sleep. But not the ministers. For them it was a day made to order for singing.

But after two hours, they were sung out. That's when one of the men got an inspired idea. He got the guide's microphone and announced to the group that we were going to have a joke telling contest. There was only one rule. The joke had to be a true story about something funny that had really happened in our respective ministries.

The next hour I never laughed so hard in my life. Their stories proved beyond a shadow of a doubt that there is never a dull moment when you're serving the Lord. When all the stories had been told and we had regained our wits (no pun intended), we decided to vote to select the best story. The stories that placed first and second were both yarns about incredibly embarrassing moments.

The second place story came from a Canadian pastor. He said that at his church they required a deacon to preside over each Sunday morning service, rotating this responsibility through the board of deacons. It seems that there was one deacon who was particularly vulnerable to stage fright. He was always nervously putting his foot in his mouth by misspeaking some announcement whenever he presided.

One morning when this deacon was scheduled to preside, the pastor discovered the district superintendent was going to be present. He asked the nervous deacon to work the superintendent into the service.

When it came time for the offering, the deacon announced, "We are privileged to have with us this morning our district superintendent, Dr. Du Pree. I'd like to request that Dr. Du Pray come pee over the offering." The tears rolled down my cheeks over that one!

But the grand-prize winner came from a missionary to Central America. He said that when he first felt the call to go into mission work, he made a tour of Latin America to survey mission possibilities. One of his first stops was in Buenos Aires, Argentina. Keep in mind that he knew almost no Spanish at the time.

On Sunday morning he got a taxi at his hotel and headed for church. The only problem was that he could not seem to communicate the address to the cab driver. They drove around aimlessly for a while, and all he saw resembling churches were Catholic Cathedrals. Finally, he spotted what appeared to be a Protestant church building. He stopped the taxi and went in.

The service had already started, and the place was packed out. The usher took him to the third row from the front. There was only one person between him and the preacher, a young man sitting on the second row. The service turned out to be rather formal in nature. The people kept standing up, sitting down, kneeling and then standing back up. Since the prospective missionary could not understand what was being said, he decided to watch the young man in front of him and do whatever he did.

At the end of the service the pastor returned to the pulpit and began making some statements. Suddenly, the young man stood up. Our friend immediately followed him. The church exploded with laughter. The missionary turned and looked behind him.

He and the young man were the only ones standing. He quickly sat down and prayed for the floor to open up and swallow him.

When the service dismissed, the missionary stayed in his seat, too embarrassed to move. He didn't know what he had done, but he knew it must have been something awful. Finally, the pastor came up and spoke to him in English.

"You don't speak Spanish, do you?" asked the pastor.

"That's right."

"Do you have any idea why you caused such a commotion?"

"No."

"Well," the pastor chuckled, "I announced that Sister Gonzalez had given birth yesterday to a baby boy. And I asked the proud father to stand."

Another very special group was the one that contained my Mom and Dad, my wife and my oldest daughter. What a joy it was to share with these precious family members the glories of Israel. I had been trying to get my wife to go with me for years, but she is a homebody who simply does not like to travel. But at long last I talked her into going, mainly because the trip was going to fall on our 25th wedding anniversary. So, reluctantly, she went. She loved it, and she's been anxious to get back ever since. The Lord poured out His love upon us by enabling us to celebrate 25 years together at a dinner in the city of Jerusalem.

But it was not quite as romantic as it sounds because we had a roommate — yes, a roommate! On the third day of that tour, one of the men had told me that he could not get any sleep because his 75-year-old father whom he was traveling with "snored like a B-52!"

I offered to let him room with my wife and me because the hotels always give the tour leader a suite. That meant we had a sitting-room separate from our bedroom. He promptly moved in and slept on our couch for the duration of the tour — even on the evening of our 25th anniversary.

My heart is full of wonderful memories of the Holy Land. But two in particular stand out. Both events touched me deeply.

The first was a visit to the Garden Tomb. I had a group with me. I had been there many times, and I was not expecting anything special. I was spiritually off guard, and the Lord "snook" up on me.

The usual procedure at the Garden is to listen to a brief lecture by one of the caretakers, then walk through the garden, view the crucifixion site, step into the tomb, and conclude with a communion service.

The caretakers who deliver the lectures rotate about every three or four months. Most of them are evangelical preachers from European countries, mainly England. They are always most cordial, and they never hold up a group very long.

They usually speak about five minutes explaining how the site was found, emphasizing that they cannot prove its authenticity, and making the point that the only important thing to keep in mind is that the tomb of Jesus, wherever it is, is empty. I knew the talk by heart.

That particular day, the man who came out to speak to us was a young Dutchman. In physical appearance he was ugly. He was tall and very thin, almost skeletal. He was completely bald-headed and had large ears that stuck out. His nose looked like it had been broken several times. It wandered all over his face. When he started speaking, I was startled to hear a heavy lisp. I was even more startled by what he had to say.

Instead of the usual tourist prattle, he simply said, "I want to take a moment to share with you what Jesus has done for me in my life."

I don't remember what he said after that. All I know is that I was translated into the presence of Jesus, and my heart was touched by the power of the Lord's Spirit.

When he finished, we all just sat there dumbfounded by what we had experienced. A lady next to me, who was a member of another group, turned to me and said, "You know, for the first time I think I understand why the Apostle Paul was such a powerful evangelist. I think he must have been like this man, with no strength or beauty in himself. Yet, in his weakness, the power of God was displayed." In three sentences that lady preached one of the most powerful sermons I had ever heard. All I could say was "Amen" and "Thank you, Lord."

The other memory that still plucks at my heartstrings occurred at one of the most dismal places in all the world, a place in Jerusalem called Yad Vashem. In English, we call it the Holocaust Museum. As its name indicates, it is a collection of historical artifacts which authenticate every aspect of one of man's most horrible crimes.

If you have any sensitivity at all, it is a tough place to walk through. It is arranged in chronological order. The first room records, in graphic photographs, the rise of Hitler.

The next room shows the beginnings of the Nazi persecutions of the Jews. On and on it goes, step by bloody step. Jewish shops are closed. Jews are arrested and taunted in public. Cattle cars are filled with human cargoes destined for work camps and ovens. There are films of executions. The prison clothing of adults and children is displayed, along with gold bricks made of fillings extracted from corpses.

Nothing is left to the imagination. Yet, the imagination cannot comprehend such bestiality. It is overpowering. I have seen entire groups walk through without speaking a word. I have witnessed people fainting. Others have gone hysterical. Some almost run through, not wanting to see any of the horror.

When I take a group there, I never try to keep them together as a group. It is too personal a place. I just give them a general introduction outside and then turn them loose to move through at their own rate of speed. I normally allot an hour and a half for them to get back to the bus. If they finish early, I urge them to walk down the Promenade of the Righteous, a beautiful garden area outside where trees have been planted in memory of righteous Gentiles who risked their lives to save Jews from the Holocaust. One of those trees is dedicated to Corrie ten Boom.

When I visited Yad Vashem with the group that included my family members, everything seemed to go well until it was time to depart. We counted heads, and my daughter, Ruth, 23 years old, was missing. I started searching for her, but I just couldn't find her anywhere — in the museum or outside. I went through the museum a second time but still did not see her.

As I was about to exit, I noticed a stairway was open that I had rarely seen open during regular tourist hours. I knew where it led because I had been there several times. It led to a long, narrow, dark room where individual records are stored concerning each person who perished in the Holocaust. This is a research facility that is rarely visited by tourists.

I went bounding up the stairs and peered into the dark room. At the far end I could make out the form of a person in the shadowy darkness. No one ever speaks above a whisper in this room, so I could not call out to see if it was Ruth.

I walked to the other end. It was Ruth. She was standing there holding onto a display stand with both hands. The stand had a dim light on it. The light illuminated a sample document under glass. It showed the photograph of a little girl 10 years old. The document contained her vital statistics — place of birth, parents, home address, place of arrest, place of imprisonment, date and place of execution. It read in matter-of-fact style.

Ruth was weeping. I put my arm around her and hugged her.

"Daddy," she whispered, "how could this happen?"

I couldn't speak. We just stood there, arm in arm, weeping together, staring at the picture of a child who represented six million of God's Chosen People.

13) Growing in the Lord

God is in the change business. He wants to shape and mold us into the image of His Son. He does this through the power of His Spirit working within us. His Spirit uses the Word, our prayers and our experiences.

Growth is never easy because it demands change. We don't

like to change. We get comfortable in our ruts, and we hunker down in them and refuse to climb out. Sometimes the Lord has to jar us loose by plowing the ruts with jolting experiences.

As I've revealed, I've had a lot of those experiences because I was too stubborn to let the Lord change me gently. I've experienced a lot of change and subsequent growth in seven years of evangelistic work. I have a lot of growth yet in front of me. We all do.

The Lord also uses experiences to give us insights that help us to grow. Often we are too spiritually insensitive to pick up on the insights, and the experiences are wasted. Other times, experiences that might on the surface appear inconsequential will have a profound impact simply because we had our spiritual antenna in place and were ready to receive what God had to offer.

As I look back over the wealth of experiences God has brought my way in seven years, there are two that stand out as foundational to the ministry I've been entrusted with. Both helped me to understand the importance of the message that Jesus is coming soon. One related that message to the unbeliever, the other to the believer. God used both experiences to motivate me to proclaim the message He had laid on my heart with urgency and fervor.

The experience that related my ministry to unbelievers occurred very shortly after the ministry was established. The setting was the Cajun country of Southern Louisiana.

I was holding a meeting at a fairly large church in Jennings, Louisiana. Following the Sunday evening service, I went to the door to greet people as they left. A young woman about 30 came up to me and enthusiastically thanked me for the message. She said she could hardly wait for the Monday evening service. I was speaking on the "Signs of the Times" that point to the soon return of Jesus. The Sunday messages had caught her imagination, and she was excited.

"I have so many questions," she said, "but I'll have to hold them till later because I've got to rush to my job."

"Oh?" I responded. "What kind of job do you have on Sunday evening?"

"I run the skating rink," she answered, "and we've got a lot of church kids coming over to skate this evening. I've got to hurry and get the place opened."

I thanked her for her kind comments and urged her not to forget her questions. She left hurriedly.

About 10:30 that evening the phone rang at the house where I was staying. I heard my host, one of the congregation's elders, suddenly exclaim, "Oh no! Oh no!" He hung up the phone and yelled at me, "Get your coat. We've got to go to the hospital."

As we tore across town in his truck, he explained that the call had been about the young woman who managed the skating rink. She had been skating with the kids when she suddenly dropped to the floor. She had been rushed to the hospital. The situation looked critical.

The moment we walked into the hospital lobby, we knew she was dead. Groups of youngsters and friends from the church were gathered in small groups all over the lobby and down the main hallway. Some were praying. Some were singing softly. Some were just comforting one another with hugs of reassurance.

She had suffered a massive cerebral hemorrhage. She was only 32. Death had come instantaneously. The doctor said she was probably dead before she hit the floor.

Her older sister arrived and received the terrible news. She was known as a woman of great faith. We tried to console her but she kept consoling us, reminding us that her sister was now with the Lord. She went from group to group encouraging them with the victory her sister now enjoyed.

Then her brother arrived. He was a man of the world. He had treated his sisters harshly because of their religious convictions.

When he learned of his sister's death, he was overcome with grief and guilt. He fell to the floor in a clump and began to weep and moan loudly.

His sister rushed to him, grabbed him by the shoulders and

literally lifted him off the floor. She slammed him up against the wall and held him there with her forearm. Looking directly into his eyes, she said, "Don't weep for your sister. Weep for yourself. She's in Heaven with the Lord. But if that were you in there on that table, you would be in hell!"

I was taken back by what appeared to be a brutal approach to a suffering person. But it must have had the right impact because within a year that brother had accepted the Lord.

I started moving up and down the hallway from group to group, praying with them and trying as best as I knew how to offer some consoling words. Suddenly, a side door flew open and in came two paramedics running and pushing a litter on wheels. On the stretcher was a man who looked to be 60. He was dressed in a tuxedo. They wheeled him into an emergency room.

A few minutes later a large entourage of "beautiful people" arrived, all dressed in tuxedos and evening gowns. They gathered outside the emergency room doors and waited for word. I learned they had been partying at a night club and that the man had collapsed on the dance floor. They thought he had suffered a heart attack.

They were right. The doctor stepped into the hallway and delivered the grim news. The man was dead from a heart attack. They all stood there for a moment in a daze, and then they turned on each other like a pack of wild animals.

A daughter, dressed in a red evening dress, turned to an older woman and began to shout curses at her. The woman was her mother, the widow of the man who had just died. There was no consolation from daughter to mother. Only curses and accusations.

"It's all your fault," the daughter screamed. "You're the cause of his heart attack. You've never given him anything but grief."

"Look who's talking," the mother shouted back, "the biggest slut in Southern Louisiana." It was a horrible scene. Family members cursing and blaming each other.

I was standing at a corner of the hallway. Down one corridor

I saw people cursing and clawing at each other. Down the other corridor I saw people consoling and loving one another. I saw death down one hallway. I saw life down the other. I saw the glory of dying in the Lord. And I saw the grim reality of dying with no hope.

God used that moment to impress upon my heart the desperate need that a lost and dying world has for the good news of Jesus Christ. Hebrews 2:15 says that Jesus died that He might "deliver all those who through fear of death are subject to life-long bondage." Revelation 14:13 says, "Blessed are those who die in the Lord."

The experience that related my ministry to believers took place at a mainline denominational church in Grand Prairie, Texas.

Grand Prairie is a metropolitan suburb located between Dallas and Ft. Worth. It is in an area that many refer to as "the buckle of the Bible Belt." This experience also took place in the early months of the ministry, shortly after our radio outreach had begun.

I got a call one day from a man who identified himself as a deacon of a particular church. He said some of the members there had heard my radio broadcasts and were interested in the possibility of my coming to their church on a Sunday evening to present a lesson on prophecy. He asked if I would be willing to do so. I said I would.

"There's one problem," he interjected. "We have a tough time trying to get anyone to come on Sunday evening, so you need to give us a jazzy title."

"A jazzy title?"

"That's right. We need something jazzy to attract attention and build curiosity."

I thought for a moment, and a title suddenly popped into my mind.

"What about calling my talk, 'The Future of the Late Great Planet Earth?' "

"Hey!" he said. "That's jazzy. I like it. That's what we'll call it. Now, there's one more problem."

"What's that?" I asked.

"We have a pastor who's not too hot about Bible studies. He likes to have folk singers and book reviewers. We've got to run this past him. He may not approve it."

I told him to give me a ring as soon as he knew something for sure. To my surprise he called back the very next day. He was excited. The pastor had "enthusiastically" agreed for me to come. We set the date.

When the evening arrived, I saw what the deacon meant about Sunday evening attendance. Only about 50 people showed up.

The pastor excused the light attendance to me by saying, "I don't blame them. This has been a beautiful day. I would have gone to the lake myself if I could have." It was a strange welcome for a guest speaker. The evening was to get even stranger.

The pastor called the service to order and began introducing me right off the bat. No songs or prayers. It was obvious he wanted to get the thing over with.

"We're honored to have with us Dr. David Reagan, an expert on Bible prophecy," he began. "Dr. Reagan is going to show us what a fool Hal Lindsey is . . ."

"What?" I thought to myself. "Did I hear this guy right?" I perked up and leaned forward to give him my undivided attention.

He droned on.

"There's been a lot of nonsense written recently by sensationalists like Hal Lindsey who try to scare everyone by saying that 'Jesus is coming soon.' That's a lot of nonsense and I'm glad to have Dr. Reagan here this evening to set the record straight."

I just couldn't believe what I was hearing. Was I dreaming? Had this man gone mad? Was this some sort of sick joke?

My search for some rational explanation was interrupted by applause. I was on, and I didn't know what to say. I mumbled around for a few moments in bewilderment thanking them for inviting me, and then I stopped and looked directly at the pastor.

"Pastor," I said, "I'm awfully sorry but I'm afraid there has been a terrible mistake."

"What do you mean?' he asked.

"Well, I happen to be a strong supporter of Hal Lindsey's. I think most of what he's written is right on target."

"You're right!" the pastor responded. "There's been a terrible mistake."

He thought for a moment.

"But we don't want to be impolite," he added, "so you go right ahead with your message."

I sighed with relief and asked everyone to turn to Acts, chapter 2. I wanted to start out by showing them how Peter utilized prophecy in his sermon at Pentecost.

Now when I ask people to turn to a Bible passage, I'm used to hearing the pages rustle. That's music to a preacher's ears. As I turned to the passage, I didn't hear any rustling of pages. I looked up. Everyone was just sitting there passively, staring at me.

"How many of you have a Bible with you?" I asked.

Not one hand was raised.

"OK, then let's use the pew Bibles."

"We don't have any pew Bibles," a man yelled.

"Well, we can't study Bible prophecy without Bibles," I said, "so let's find some." I asked four of the men to go through the classrooms in the educational wing of the building and gather up some Bibles. While they looked, I led the group in a couple of praise songs.

The men returned empty-handed.

"We can't find any Bibles in this church," one of them said.

The pastor jumped up and said, "I think I have a few in my office."

He returned with five Bibles. We divided the congregation into five groups and gave each group a Bible.

"OK," I said, "now turn to Acts 2." The pages started rustling. It sounded good. I started reading from Acts 2. The pages continued to rustle. I looked up. Every group was still searching for Acts! Some were at the beginning of the Bible searching through Genesis.

I was thunderstruck. I had grown up in a church that idolized the book of Acts. It was about all we ever studied. I didn't know there were Christians anywhere who could not find Acts.

I departed from Acts and conducted a Bible drill to familiarize the people with the book they had in front of them. I explained the difference between the Old Testament and the New and then we surveyed the various divisions — History, Wisdom, Prophecy, etc. The people got excited.

All of us turned to the newly discovered book of Acts, and I made my point about Peter's use of prophecy. Then I asked them to turn to Daniel.

The pastor jumped to his feet.

"Why the book of Daniel?" he asked.

"Because I want to show you a prophecy in that book about the first coming of Christ."

"But there is no prophecy in Daniel," the pastor said. "The book of Daniel is a fraud. It shouldn't even be in the Bible. It is history written like prophecy to make it sell better. It claims to have been written about 500 B.C., when in reality it was written about 100 years before Christ."

Now keep in mind that this pastor is standing in front of his congregation publicly heaping scorn and ridicule on one of the books of the Bible. I was biting my tongue, trying to refrain from giving him some sort of scathing, sarcastic reply.

He continued. "You can quote from any other book except Daniel. But I don't allow Daniel to be quoted in this church."

Then he got personal and said, "You obviously are not a seminary graduate because no seminary graduate would ever stoop to quote Daniel."

My blood was boiling. I wanted to say something cute like, "I'm not a cemetery graduate, if that's what you mean." But I prayed for self-control, and the Spirit prevailed. I decided to challenge him but to do so as politely as possible.

"If Daniel was written only a hundred years before Christ, how do you explain its inclusion in the Septuagint?"

"What do you mean?" he asked.

"I mean the Septuagint was translated around 250 B.C. Daniel was included in that translation, so Daniel had to be written before that time."

"I don't believe that's when the Septuagint was translated," he responded.

"OK, then how do you explain the fact that when Alexander the Great came to Jerusalem in 333 BC, he decided to spare the city because the High Priest showed him where he was prophesied in Daniel?"

"Where did you come across that crazy story?" the pastor asked.

"It's in the writings of Josephus."

"Then it's nothing but a legend," he snapped, "because Josephus never wrote anything except old wives' tales."

"Maybe I should just go home," I replied.

"Oh no," said the pastor, "you go right ahead with your presentation. Just don't quote from Daniel."

I should have stopped. But I tried to continue.

"Let's take a look at the very first prophecy in the Bible. Everyone turn to Genesis 3:15."

Instantly the pastor was back on his feet.

"Come on, Dr. Reagan," he said, " you're not going to start talking about myths like the virgin birth, are you?"

So it went, all evening long. A man responsible for the care and feeding of a flock of 300 people kept jumping up to ridicule the Word of God and the fundamental truths it reveals.

I wish I could say this is an isolated experience. It is not. I've had many like it since that time.

God used this experience to open my eyes to the dreadful condition of the contemporary church. He showed me the apathy and apostasy that have sapped the church of its vitality and dynamism. He showed me the overwhelming need for revival and spiritual renewal. He let me see the meaning of Paul's prophecy in II Timothy 3:5 where he wrote that in the end times the church "will have the form of religion but will deny its power" (RSV).

Believe it or not, the Lord showed me something else in this experience. He once again revealed His great sense of humor. You may be wondering how I came to that conclusion.

It relates to how I was invited in the first place. Several months later I ran into the deacon who had called me. I asked him how he ever got the pastor to approve my invitation when he so obviously disagreed with my viewpoint.

"It was a remarkable coincidence!" he said.

He explained that the morning he went to the pastor's office to clear my invitation, the pastor was sitting at his desk reading a book. The book was entitled, "The Future of the Late Great Planet Earth." I had never heard of the book, yet that was exactly the "jazzy" title that the Spirit had led me to give my proposed talk. The book contained a scathing denunciation of Hal Lindsey and his prophetic concepts. When the deacon told the pastor my proposed topic, the pastor assumed I had pulled the title from that book and that I agreed with the book!

The Lord has worked in equally hilarious ways many times to open doors for me that would never have been opened otherwise. God has a great sense of humor, and the results are not "coincidences." They are "God-incidences."

Part III:

The Message
"Living on Borrowed Time"

1) Knowing the Season

Twenty years ago if you had asked me, "Can we know when the Lord will return?" I would have answered with an emphatic, dogmatic "No!"

But after 20 years of studying God's Prophetic Word, I have come to a different conclusion. Now, my answer would be "Yes and No." No, we cannot know the date of the Lord's return. We can't know the year or month or day. But, yes, we can know the season — and the exciting news is that we are living in that season!

Now by a "season" I don't mean a period of three months, nor do I mean a particularly short period of years. Keep in mind that Noah preached for 120 years that the people of his time were living in the season of the pouring out of God's wrath.

I'm sure that after preaching that message for five years, people wrote him off as a "one issue obsessionist." And I'm certain that after half a century of preaching the same message, people laughed and jeered and reminded him that he had been saying the same thing for 50 years. Some probably kept on laughing until they couldn't tread water anymore.

But Noah was right, and he got the last laugh. They truly

were living in the season of God's wrath, and the wrath of God could have been poured out on them at any time after Noah issued his first warning.

I often encounter the same kind of scoffing among Christian people today when I talk about the soon coming of Jesus. Some laugh. Others write me off as nuts. Some get hostile. Others are just cantankerous.

One of the most common comments I receive is, "I've heard all that before." Once a crusty old farmer came up to me after a sermon on the signs of the times. He patted me on the shoulder in a condescending manner and said, "That was really nice, son, but I heard that stuff back in World War I when I was a kid."

"Praise God!" I responded. "You need to thank God for growing up under a Bible-believing preacher."

What that man did not realize is that his boyhood preacher was right on target because we have been in the season of the Lord's return ever since the beginning of World War I. God worked through that war's evil to initiate His end time program, for that war resulted in the land of Israel being transferred from a people who hated the Jews — the Turks — to a people who were sympathetic to the Jews — the British. The first thing the British did was to issue the Balfour Declaration in which they declared that Palestine should become a homeland for the Jews.

But the Jews did not return to that land in large numbers. They had become acculturated to their adopted nations. They had to be motivated to return to their ancestral land. That motivation came with the Holocaust of World War II. The Jews emerged from that nightmare saying, "Never again! Never again! We will have our own land and our own state. Never again will we submit ourselves to another Hitler." Millions began to stream back to Palestine from the ends of the earth.

Old Testament prophecy always presents the return of the Lord at a time when the Jew is back in the land. The Old Testament prophets speak repeatedly of the fact that in the end times the Jews will return in unbelief to their homeland, and the nation of Israel will be reestablished (See Ezekiel 37).

God has the wisdom and power to orchestrate all the evil of man and Satan to the triumph of Jesus. He proved that by converting the Cross into a triumph. Likewise, God was able to work through the evil of World Wars I and II to bring about His own good purposes. He used World War I to prepare the land of Israel for the Jews. He used World War II to prepare the Jews for the land of Israel.

The moment I start telling people that we can know the season of the Lord's return, I always get the same scripture thrown at me, "Jesus is coming like a thief in the night." I know exactly how those who use that scripture feel. I grew up in a church that put no emphasis on prophetic teaching concerning the second coming. Every time someone would ask a question about the return of the Lord, they would be put down with the words, "Jesus is coming like a thief in the night."

Because that was the only prophetic scripture I knew, I drew the conclusion that there was nothing we could know about the timing of the Lord's return. He was going to sneak up on us like a thief and catch us unaware. Therefore, it was a waste of time to worry about when He would return. I put the whole matter out of my mind and became apathetic about the return of Jesus.

You can imagine how shocked I was when I started studying Bible prophecy and one of the first discoveries which the Spirit led me to was the fact that this famous scripture about the Lord returning as a thief *does not apply to Christians!* The Bible says so point blank.

Let's look at I Thessalonians, chapters 4 and 5. Chapter 4 ends with a detailed description of the Rapture of the Church. Chapter 5 begins with a statement about the timing of this end time event: "Now as to the times and the epochs, brethren, you have no need of anything to be written to you. For you yourselves know full well that the day of the Lord will come just like a thief in the night." (verses 1 and 2)

There it is, the famous statement that the Lord will return like a thief.

But keep reading: "But you, brethren, are not in darkness, that the day should overtake you like a thief." (verse 4)

How could anything be clearer? Jesus is going to return like a thief in the night — that is, suddenly and unexpectedly — except for the "brethren."

This means that the return of Jesus will be a shocking surprise to the world — to those who have rejected Him. But it should be no surprise to those who have accepted Him in faith. He is not coming for Christians as a thief in the night.

But how can Christians know the season of His return? The next two verses tell us: "For you are all sons of light and sons of day. We are not of night nor of darkness; so then let us not sleep as others do, but let us be alert and sober" (verses 5 and 6).

We can know the season of the Lord's return because we are "children of light."

What does this mean?

I think it is a reference to the indwelling Spirit of God. All true Christians are indwelt by the Spirit (Rom. 8:14). The Spirit opens our eyes and enlightens our minds so that we can understand the mysteries of God's Word (I Cor. 2:6-12 and I John 2:27). In other words, if we will read the Word, and believe the Word, the Spirit will help us understand the Word, and through that understanding we can recognize the season of the Lord's return.

What I'm saying is that there is no excuse for the return of the Lord to catch any Christian by surprise. Yet, tragically, many professing Christians will be caught by surprise, like a thief in the night, because they either do not read the Word or do not believe it or do not rely upon the Spirit to explain it.

There's another reason we can know the season of the Lord's return. It's because God is obligated to reveal the season to us. That's right. *God is obligated to let us know the season of His Son's return.* You ask, "Why?" It's because of the nature of God's character.

Let me put it this way: God would violate His character if He were to send Jesus Christ back without any warning. Since God cannot violate His own character, He is obligated to warn us before Jesus returns.

This point raises a further question: "Why is God obligated to warn us of Jesus' return?" The answer is simple. It is because Jesus is returning in wrath, and the Bible teaches from beginning to end that God never pours out His wrath without warning because God does not wish that any should perish but that all should come to repentance.

Consider the points carefully:

1) Jesus is returning in wrath. He is coming to pour out the wrath of God upon those who have rejected the grace and mercy of God (I Thess. 1:10).

2) God does not wish that any should perish but that all should come to repentance (II Peter 3:9).

3) Therefore, God must warn before Jesus returns, just as He has always warned before He has poured out His wrath (II Peter 2:4-10).

God warned through Noah before He poured out His wrath upon all the earth. God warned through Abraham before He destroyed Sodom and Gomorrah. Likewise, the Bible says God will warn all the earth through an angel before He pours out His final bowls of wrath at the end of the Tribulation period (Rev. 14:6-7). Since the entire Tribulation will be a time of wrath, God must warn before that period begins and He sends His Son for the Church.

2) Recognizing the Season

How can we recognize the season? What are we to look for? The Bible tells us to be alert for "signs of the times."

It is a principle that applied to the first coming of Jesus, and we can learn from its application there. Look at Matthew 16. The chapter begins with Jesus being tested by the Scribes and Pharisees. They asked Him to prove that He was the Messiah by performing a sign — or a miracle.

Jesus answered them sarcastically: "When it is evening, you say, 'It will be fair weather, for the sky is red.' And in the morning, 'There will be a storm today, for the sky is red and threatening.' Do you know how to discern the appearance of the sky but cannot discern the signs of the times?" (verses 2 and 3).

Jesus says, "I don't understand you guys. You can read the weather signs but you can't read the signs of the times!" What did Jesus mean by the term, "signs of the times"?

I think He was referring to Old Testament prophecies. There are more than 300 of those prophecies or signs, and they reveal every aspect of the nature and being of the Messiah. They tell that he will be born of the lineage of Abraham and David, that He will be born in Bethlehem of a virgin, that He will go into Egypt, that He will reside in Galilee, and that He will be a prophet, teacher and healer.

Now think about it — these Scribes and Pharisees had spent their lives studying these signs. They knew them by heart. Yet, they were so spiritually blind that they could not recognize the One who was fulfilling those signs before their eyes.

Likewise, the Bible contains many signs about the second advent of the Messiah. In fact, there are many more prophecies about the second coming than there are about the first. There are over 500 prophecies in the Old Testament about the second coming of the Lord and, in the New Testament, one out of every 25 verses focuses on that event.

There are, in fact, so many signs given concerning the second coming of Jesus that it is hard to get a handle on them. I've tried to do so by sorting them into broad categories.

Here are the categories I've come up with:

1) The Signs of Nature — earthquakes, famines, pestilence and signs in the heavens.
2) The Signs of Society — immorality, lawlessness, violence, humanism, materialism, hedonism and despair.
3) The Spiritual Signs — there are negative ones like cults, satanism and the apostasy of the professing church. There are positive ones like the worldwide preaching of the Gospel, the pouring out of the Holy Spirit and prophetic illumination — that is, the understanding of Bible prophecy.
4) The Signs of Technology — these include Biblical prophecies that can only be explained by the development of lasers, computers, aircraft and nuclear weapons.
5) The Signs of World Politics — the emergence of Russia and China as major world powers, the consolidation of Europe into a loose confederation of states, and the world armaments race.
6) The Signs of Israel — the regathering of the Jews, the reestablishment of the state of Israel, the revival of the Hebrew language, the reclamation of the land, and the reoccupation of the city of Jerusalem.

The specific signs within each of these broad categories are numerous. I've only named a few to give you a feel for each category.

One of the most comprehensive and detailed passages in the Bible regarding these signs of the second coming is one that Jesus Himself spoke during the last week of His life. It is often referred to as "The Olivet Discourse" because He delivered the speech to His disciples while they were sitting on the Mt. of Olives, looking down at the Temple Mount. The speech is recorded in Matthew 24, Mark 13 and Luke 21.

It is in reality a double prophecy, referring in part to the destruction of Jerusalem by the Romans in 70 A.D., but referring ultimately to the destruction Jerusalem will suffer right before the return of the Lord at the end of this age. This is something characteristic of Bible prophecies. They often have a prefillment in type before they experience their ultimate fulfillment.

There can be no doubt that the Olivet Discourse was not fulfilled in 70 A.D. In Matthew 24 it is recorded that Jesus said the signs to be watched for would precede the greatest tribulation ever to be experienced by the Jewish people (verse 21). The destruction of Jerusalem in 70 A.D, as terrible as it was, with the loss of a million Jewish lives, was nothing compared to the Nazi Holocaust. The Holocaust will pale in comparison to what the Jews will suffer at the hands of the Anti-Christ during the Tribulation. The prophet Zechariah says that during that time two-thirds of the Jews will perish (Zech. 13:8).

In Matthew 24:22 the Lord says that the signs will precede a period so terrible that His return will be the only thing that will prevent mankind from destroying itself. That was not true in 70 A.D. In fact, we are living in the only period in history where that prophecy could come literally true because of the development of nuclear weapons.

Also, Jesus says that the signs He outlines will precede a period that will climax with His return: "But immediately after the tribulation of those days the sun will be darkened, and the moon will not give its light, and the stars will fall from the sky, and the powers of the heavens will be shaken, and then the sign of the Son of Man will appear in the sky, and then all the tribes of the earth will mourn, and they will see the Son of Man coming on the clouds of the sky with power and great glory" (verses 29 and 30).

Notice He says, "immediately." It has been almost 2,000 years since Titus destroyed Jerusalem. The Lord did not return then. The signs of Matthew 24 are yet to be fulfilled.

Let's look at those signs. I think it's significant that Jesus begins with a spiritual sign — the emergence of false Christs (verse 5). I think it is also significant that this is the only sign He repeats, and He repeats it twice, in verses 11 and 24. In the latter verse He warns of false Christs who will even be able to perform miracles. I think it is no coincidence that the world has experienced a literal epidemic of cultic groups since the mid-1800s and that today many of those cults are able to perform miracles by the power of Satan.

In verses 6 and 7 Jesus shifts to the signs of world politics. He speaks of wars and rumors of wars, of nation rising against nation and kingdom against kingdom (civil war).

We live in that age. The period since the end of World War II has been the most violent period of "peace" in the history of Man. There are over 40 wars and civil wars going on in the world today. Over 200,000 lives have been lost in four of them — Iran-Iraq, Cambodia, Lebanon and Afghanistan.

In verse seven Jesus also mentions signs of nature — famines and earthquakes. Luke's account adds pestilence and signs in the heavens (Luke 21:11). There is probably no category of signs with less respect than the signs of nature. People respond, "But there's always been earthquakes and famines. What else is new?" But note what Jesus says in verse eight of Matthew 24. He says the signs of nature will be like "birth pangs."

Now, I have never experienced birth pangs, so I asked my wife what this means. She said it was "obvious." She explained that when birth pangs begin they increase in two ways the closer you get to the actual birth. They increase in frequency and intensity. In other words, the closer we get to the coming of the Lord, there will be more earthquakes and more intense ones. The same will be true of famine and pestilence and the other signs of nature.

In verses 9 and 10 Jesus shifts back to spiritual signs — the persecution of believers and the apostasy of the church. Some will fall away because of persecution (verse 10). Others will depart from the faith because of the deception of false prophets (verse 11). And others will forsake the Lord because they will get caught up in the lawlessness of society (verse 12).

The Lord's mention of lawlessness in verse 12 is not His only reference to the signs of society. He focuses on this category in verses 37-39 where He says that society will evolve full circle and will take on the characteristics of Noah's corrupt civilization. People will be living it up, their hearts hardened against God and their lives given to the pursuit of pleasure.

Most important, the Lord emphasized the signs of Israel. He says that His return will take place at a time when the Jews are back in the land, their temple has been rebuilt, and their sacrificial system has been reinstituted (verses 15-20). Although there is not one prophecy that must be fulfilled for the Lord to come for His Church, there are some that must be fulfilled before the Lord returns to reign. Two are mentioned in this passage — the rebuilding of the Temple and the reinstitution of the Mosaic system of sacrifice. The third prophecy mentioned here, the return of the Jews to the land, has been fulfilled in this century.

Matthew 24 is just one of many detailed passages in both the Old and New Testaments which outline signs we are to watch for, signs that will alert us to the Lord's return. If you will believe these and watch for them, the Lord's return will not catch you "like a thief in the night."

3) Understanding the Urgency of the Season

God worked through World War I to put His end time program into effect. We have been in the season of the Lord's return ever since that time.

But there is an important point yet to be made. The signs of Israel indicate that we are near the end of the season, that Jesus is at the very gate of Heaven, and that we are living on borrowed time.

The Signs of Israel are more important than all the rest of the signs put together. The reason for this is that the Jewish people are God's prophetic time clock. God always links major prophecies to events that will occur in the history of the Jewish nation.

Let me give you two examples. There are two Old Testament prophecies which nail down the time period of the Lord's first advent. Both relate that advent to events in Jewish history. The first of these prophecies is found in Genesis 49:10 where Jacob said to his son Judah, "The scepter shall not depart from Judah, nor the ruler's staff from between his feet, until Shiloh comes, and to him shall be the obedience of the peoples."

"Shiloh" is a recognized Messianic title. What this prophecy says is that Judah will not lose its ruling power before the Messiah comes. Judah lost its ruling power in about 7 A.D. when the Romans removed the power of the Sanhedrin Council to apply the death penalty. Jewish history records that on that day the High Priest put on sack cloth and ashes and wept over the fact that "the scepter has passed from Judah and Shiloh has not come." But Shiloh had come, for Jesus had been born in 4 B.C., and He was to begin His ministry in 27 A.D.

The second Old Testament passage that uses Jewish historical events to set the season of the Lord's first coming is found in Daniel 9:24-27. Here Daniel prophesies that the Messiah will be "cut off" 69 weeks of years after the issuance of a command to rebuild Jerusalem. The command was issued by Artaxerxes in 445 B.C., and 69 weeks of years later (483 lunar years), Jesus was crucified in Jerusalem.

If the Bible contains two such specific prophecies concerning the season of the Lord's first coming, I think it is only logical to assume that there must be prophecies which narrow down the season of His second coming, particularly when you keep in mind the fact that He will return in wrath, necessitating God's warning.

I want to show you three such prophecies which link Jewish historical events to the return of Jesus. All three point to the period in which we are living. I'm going to start with the broadest and most general and conclude with the most specific.

The first is found in Hosea 5 and 6. Here's the whole passage as it appears in the New American Standard Version:

> *I will go away and return to My place*
> *Until they acknowledge their guilt and seek my*
> *   face;*
> *In their affliction they will earnestly seek Me.*
> *"Come let us return to the Lord.*
> *For He has torn us but He will heal us;*
> *He has wounded us but He will bandage us,*
> *He will revive us after two days;*
> *He will raise us up on the third day*
> *That we may live before Him."*
>
> Hosea 5:15-6:2

Hosea says a time will come when the Lord will return to His place — that is, Heaven. The Lord will remain there until "they" — the Jewish people — confess their guilt and seek His face. We know from other Old Testament passages (for example, Zechariah 12:10) that the Jews will not turn to the Lord until the end of the Tribulation. They will have to have their hardened hearts pounded by the wrath of man, Satan and God before they will repent. The next clause affirms that the repentance will occur during the Tribulation. Hosea says the Jews will cry out to God "in their affliction" at a time when they have been "torn" and "wounded." Then the Lord will bind them up and revive them.

When will this take place? The passage gives the timing. It will occur "after two days." In II Peter 3:8 and Psalm 90:4 we are told that to the Lord, a thousand years is like a day. Is that the meaning here? I think so because the next clause says that at the end of the two days, the Lord will "raise us up" to live before Him "on the third day." This appears to be a reference to the resurrection of Jewish believers that will take place at the end of the Tribulation (Dan.12:1-2). Living before the Lord on the third day appears to be a reference to the 1,000-year reign of Jesus (Rev. 20:1-6).

So Hosea is saying that the Jews, as a nation, will repent and accept Jesus as their Messiah at the end of a two thousand year period which will be followed by the millennial rule of Jesus. We are at the end of that 2,000-year period. We are living on borrowed time.

The second timing prophecy is found in Matthew 24:32-36, in the middle of Jesus' Olivet Discourse. Have you ever noticed that prior to these verses everything He says in that speech is presented in matter-of-fact, one-two-three form? He says this event will happen and then that event and then some other event. But when we get to verse 32, the Lord suddenly shifts gears and moves into mystery language. He suddenly inserts a parable.

"Now learn the parable from the fig tree: when its branch has already become tender and puts forth its leaves, you know that summer is near; even so you too, when you see all these things, recognize that He is near, right at the door. Truly I say to you, this generation will not pass away until all these things take place" (Matthew 24:32-34).

Now why did the Lord shift to symbolic language in verse 32? Why did He interject this parable? A lot of people have a mistaken idea about parables. They think Jesus used parables to make things simpler to understand. That is not true. Jesus used parables to make things harder to understand. He cloaked great insights in parables so that only those who have the Holy Spirit can understand (See Mark 4:10-12).

Accordingly, I believe Jesus shifted to the symbolic language of a parable at this point in His speech because He wanted to give believers a clue to the timing of His return. The clue is "the fig tree." This is one of several symbols of Israel that is used in Old Testament prophecy (See Hosea 9:10, Jer. 24:1-10 and Joel 1:7).

But why the fig tree? Do you remember what had happened on the previous day? Jesus and His disciples were walking over the Mt. of Olives when Jesus suddenly stopped and put a curse on a barren fig tree. The tree withered (Matt. 21:18ff). What was that all about? Jesus was using the fig tree as a symbol of

Israel. Like the barren tree, Israel had no spiritual fruit. The Jews had rejected their Messiah. The curse on the tree and its withering was a symbolic prophecy of the wrath of God that would fall on the Jews.

Now, on the next day, Jesus says, "Remember the fig tree? Watch it. When it blooms again, all these things I've been talking about will take place." For the past four hundred years prophetic scholars have pointed to this passage and have urged us to watch for the reestablishment of Israel. And for four hundred years most people, including Christians, have laughed and scoffed and ridiculed because they did not believe that the nation of Israel would ever exist again.

But the laughing stopped on May 14, 1948, when the independence of the state of Israel was proclaimed to the world. Israel, as prophesied, once more became a reality in the face of incredible odds. The rebirth of that nation is one of the surest signs that we are living on borrowed time.

One note — many people misread what Jesus said in this parable. They think the parable says that the Lord will return within one generation of the rebirth of Israel. Since the Bible often identifies a generation as 40 years, people have jumped to the conclusion that the Lord must come for His Church before the end of 1988.

The parable does not say the Lord will return within 40 years of Israel's rebirth. It says that the generation that sees the reestablishment of Israel is the generation that will see all the end time events come to pass. "Generation" here is used generically, like we would use it in reference to the "Beat Generation" or the "Rock Generation."

I think the parable means that someone who was alive on May 14, 1948, will be alive when the Lord returns. That may be a person who was a six-month-old babe in 1948 and will be 70 years old when the Lord comes back. The point is that the word "generation" does not tie the prophecy down to a fulfillment within a 40-year period. But it does narrow the period. And we are in that period. Again, we are living on borrowed time.

The third prophecy that helps set the season of the Lord's return is the most specific of all. It is also the one that convinces me the most that we are living in that season. It is found in Luke's account of the Olivet Discourse. "... they will fall by the edge of the sword and will be led captive into all the nations; and Jerusalem will be trampled under foot by the Gentiles until the times of the Gentiles be fulfilled" (Luke 21:24).

In the first half of this prophecy, Jesus says that the Jews will be conquered and led captive among the nations. They were conquered in 70 A.D. by the Romans, and in the years that followed, they were dispersed over the face of the earth, just as Jesus prophesied.

Now look at the second half of this prophecy. Jesus said Jerusalem will be trodden down by the Gentiles "until the times of the Gentiles are fulfilled." The Romans were the first Gentile nation to take Jerusalem following the pronouncement of the prophecy. They were followed by the Byzantines. The Byzantines were followed by the Arabs; the Arabs by the Crusaders; the Crusaders by the Mamelukes; the Mamelukes by the Turks; the Turks by the British; and the British by the Jordanians.

Jerusalem was "trampled by the Gentiles" from 70 A.D. until 1967. On June 7, 1967, during the Six Day War, the old city of Jerusalem was conquered by the Israelis. The Jews were back in control of their sacred City of David for the first time in 1,897 years.

On the day Jerusalem was retaken, the Jewish commandos rushed to the Wailing Wall to pray. As some shouted praises and others wept, Rabbi Shlomo Goren, the chief rabbi of the Israeli Army, came up to the wall in his army fatigues, blew a ram's horn and lifted his right hand, signaling for silence. He then said, "I proclaim to you the beginning of the Messianic Age." The Orthodox Jews understand the significance of the season we are living in. They are watching for the appearance of the Messiah any moment. They will not be surprised by His coming. They will be surprised only by the nail prints in His hands.

The Christian Age began with an overlap period. The Church was established in 30 A.D. on the Day of Pentecost. It wasn't until 40 years later that God set aside His Chosen People, the Jews, by allowing the Romans to conquer Jerusalem. Since June of 1967 we have been in a similar overlap period. The Age is drawing to a close. God is preparing to take the Church out of this world and pick up where He left off with the Jews to accomplish all His purposes in history and to prepare the way for the reign of His Son.

We are living on borrowed time.

4) Responding to the Season

The message of the soon coming of Jesus is like a two-edged sword. It cuts both ways. It is both good news and bad.

For those who have never accepted Jesus as their Lord and Savior, the news of His soon return is bad indeed. For them, Jesus will return as their "Holy Terror," for He is coming to pour out the incredible wrath of God upon those who have rejected God's grace and mercy.

This is the paradox of Jesus. He is both God's grace and wrath. He came the first time as a suffering lamb to die for the sins of Mankind. He is returning as a conquering lion to take retribution on those who have rejected His sacrifice.

The return of Jesus in wrath is one of the best kept secrets in Christendom. The Church has long proclaimed, as it should, the love that God expressed in Jesus. But the Church has neglected to teach that Jesus will return in wrath. It is not a pleasant message. Satan does not want it proclaimed. He has succeeded in cowering the Church into timidity. The result is that the world is ignorant of the coming wrath, as are most Christians.

Satan has convinced most people that God is the "Cosmic Teddy Bear," that He is a warm, cuddly figure who is full of only love. They imagine that when they stand before Him, He will put His arm around them and wink at their sins and ignore the fact that they never accepted the gift of love that He gave in His Son.

God is full of love. But God is also holy and righteous. He cannot countenance sin. Because of His love, He has provided Mankind with a sin covering — the blood of His Son, Jesus. Because of His righteousness, He must deal with those who reject that covering. He will do so when He sends His Son back to this earth.

The Bible says that Jesus is coming "to judge and make war." (Rev. 19:11).

The Bible says that the politicians of the world will get on their knees and cry out for the rocks and mountains to fall upon them, so fierce will be the wrath of Jesus (Rev. 6:15-17).

The Bible says that on the day of the Lord's return the blood of those who have sinned against God will be poured out like dust (Zeph. 1:17).

The Bible says the Day of the Lord will be one of "trouble and distress, destruction and desolation, darkness and gloom," a day when sinners will stagger about like blind men (Zeph. 1:15 and 17).

The Bible says that sinners will be thrown into "the great wine press of the wrath of God" — and their very life will be squeezed out of them (Rev. 14:19).

The Bible says, "The Lord is good, a stronghold in the day of trouble and He knows those who take refuge in Him." But the same passage also says, "A jealous and avenging God is the Lord; the Lord is avenging and wrathful. The Lord takes vengeance on His adversaries, and He reserves wrath for His enemies. The Lord is slow to anger and great in

power, and the Lord will by no means leave the guilty un-
punished." (Zeph. 1:7, 2-3)

God does not wish that any should perish (II Peter 3:9), but
God demands repentance (Joel 2:12-13) and the acceptance of
the grace that He has expressed through Jesus Christ (Rom.
10:9). If you have never accepted Jesus as your Lord and Savior, you need to get on your knees before God, confess your
sins, and ask Jesus to come into your heart that you might be
born again and have the hope of eternal life (John 3:3 and 16). If
you do this, then you need to seek out a fellowship of believers
where you can witness your faith in Jesus through baptism and
where you can be discipled in the Lord.

The message of the season for the sinner is flee from the
wrath that is to come by fleeing into the loving arms of Jesus
Christ.

There is also a message in the second coming of Jesus for
those who have accepted Him and have been born again. God is
calling them to commitment and holiness.

With regard to commitment, the Church today is full of Christians who have accepted Jesus as Savior but have never accepted
Him as Lord. The reason is simple. To accept Him as Savior is
free. His saving grace is a gift of God. But to accept Him as
Lord requires a price. It means putting your hand to the plow
and never looking back (Luke 9:62). It means becoming a disci-
ple of the Lord and not just a cheerleader. It means making Jesus Lord of everything in your life — the books you read, the
movies you see, the music you listen to, the TV programs you
watch, the hobbies you spend time on, the thoughts you culti-
vate, and the job you work at.

This Lordship of Jesus is tied inextricably to the second thing
God is calling believers to. He is calling us to holiness. Jesus is
coming for His Bride, the Church. He wants a Bride that is
clean and pure — one that is in the world but not of the world;
one that is the salt of the earth, standing for righteousness.

The Church today is full of secular Christians whose Christianity is a cultural thing rather than a radical lifestyle separated

from the world. Too many Christians are walking with one foot in the Church and the other in the country club. The only way the world even knows that most of us are Christians is the fact that we go to church on Sunday morning. The rest of the week we live like pagans — cheating on our wives, cheating our business partners, cheating our customers, and cheating the government on our income tax.

God is calling Christians to stop playing church. He wants us to stop filling our lives with garbage. He wants to fill us, instead, with His Spirit.

> The Bible says to believers: "The night is almost gone and the day is at hand. Let us therefore lay aside the deeds of darkness and put on the armor of light. Let us behave properly as in the day, not in carousing and drunkenness, not in sexual promiscuity and sensuality, not in strife and jealousy. But put on the Lord Jesus Christ and make no provision for the flesh in regard to lusts" (Rom. 13:12-14).

> The Bible says that believers are "to deny ungodliness and worldly desires and to live sensibly, righteously and godly in the present age" as they await the return of the Lord (Titus 2:12).

> The Bible says to believers who are awaiting Christ: "Gird your minds for action, keep sober in spirit, fix your hope completely on the grace to be brought to you at the revelation of Jesus Christ. As obedient children, do not be conformed to the former lusts which were yours in your ignorance, but like the Holy One who called you, be holy yourselves also in all your behavior; because it is written, 'You shall be holy, for I am holy' " (I Peter 1:13-15).

Believer, have you accepted Jesus as Lord? Have you committed your life to holiness? All of it? Have you presented your body as a living sacrifice, holy and acceptable to God? (Rom. 12:1) If not, you too need to repent. You need to call upon God to fill you with His Spirit so that Jesus can be the Lord of all your life (Luke 11:13).

I want to close with some incredibly good news. It is the

news that for those who put their trust in Jesus as the Christ, the Anointed One of God, the return of Jesus will be a blessed day, not a day of fear and darkness and terror. For to those who have been born again, Jesus is the "Blessed Hope" (Titus 2:13), for He is coming "to deliver us from the wrath that is to come" (I Thess. 1:10).

Hallelujah! And Maranatha!

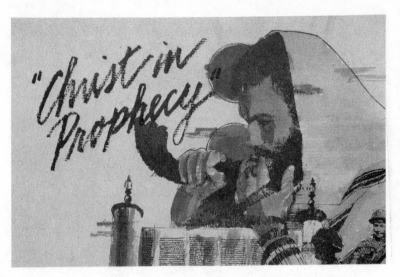

A dramatic video series on Bible prophecy
featuring
Dr. David R. Reagan

Six lessons on the fundamentals of Bible prophecy. Each lesson is 55 minutes long. Filmed before a live audience and includes questions and answers.